The Soldier and Social Change

SAGE SERIES ON ARMED FORCES AND SOCIETY

INTER-UNIVERSITY SEMINAR ON ARMED FORCES AND SOCIETY

Morris Janowitz, *University of Chicago*
Chairman and Series Editor

Charles C. Moskos, Jr., *Northwestern University*
Associate Chairman and Series Editor

Also in this series:

Vol. I   HANDBOOK OF MILITARY INSTITUTIONS
        Edited by Roger W. Little

Vol. II   MILITARY PROFESSIONALIZATION AND POLITICAL POWER
        by Bengt Abrahamsson

Vol. III MILITARY INSTITUTIONS AND THE SOCIOLOGY OF WAR:
        A Review of the Literature with Annotated Bibliography
        by Kurt Lang

Vol. IV THE UNITED STATES ARMY IN TRANSITION
        by Zeb B. Bradford, Jr. and Frederic J. Brown

Vol. V   SOLDIERS AND KINSMEN IN UGANDA:
        The Making of a Military Ethnocracy
        by Ali A. Mazrui

Vol. VI SOCIOLOGY AND THE MILITARY ESTABLISHMENT
        Third Edition
        by Morris Janowitz
        in collaboration with
        Roger W. Little

Vol. VII THE SOLDIER AND SOCIAL CHANGE
        by Jacques van Doorn

THE SOLDIER

AND

SOCIAL CHANGE

COMPARATIVE STUDIES IN THE HISTORY AND SOCIOLOGY OF THE MILITARY

Jacques van Doorn

 SAGE PUBLICATIONS   Beverly Hills / London

For information address:
SAGE Publications, Ltd.
St. Georges House
44 Hatton Garden
London, EC1.

SAGE Publications, Inc.
275 South Beverly Drive
Beverly Hills
California 90212

International Standard Book Number 0-8039-9948-8
Library of Congress Catalog Card No. 74-31573

First Printing
Printed in the United States of America

CONTENTS

Preface   vii
   MORRIS JANOWITZ

I: THE EMERGENCE OF THE MODERN MILITARY

1. The Genesis of Military and Industrial Organization   5
   Introduction
   The Early Pattern of Organization
   The Emergence of Formal Organization
   The Technical Revolution

2. The Officer Corps: A Fusion of Profession and
      Organization   29
   Introduction
   The Rise of Military Organization
   Professionalization of the Officership
   The Fusion of Profession and Organization
   Conclusions

II: THE MILITARY IN MODERN SOCIETY

3. The Decline of the Mass Army   51
   Introduction
   The Mass Army: Size, Homogeneity, Mobilization
   The End of the Draft?
   A State within the State?

4. Political Change and the Control of the Military   65
   Introduction
   Findings
   Discussion
   Conclusions

5. The Military and the Crisis of Legitimacy   87
   Introduction
   Conceptual Clarification
   The Legitimate Political Order and the Armed Forces
   The Legitimation of Violence and the Armed Forces

III: EXECUTION AND CONTROL OF FORCE

6. Justifying Military Action:
      The Dutch Return to Indonesia 1945-49   111
   "Mission Interrupted"
   Patterns of Ideology
   Hard Facts and Selective Perception
   Sources of Ideology

7. Use of Violence in Counter Insurgency:
      The Indonesian Scene 1945-49   133
   Current Fictions
   The Armed Forces in Command
   Types of Violence
   Point of No Return

ACKNOWLEDGEMENTS   179

INDEX   183

PREFACE

This volume presents the outstanding contributions of Jacques van Doorn to the study of military organization and the role of the military in socio-political change. For over a decade he has consistently and energetically pursued the study of the soldier as a social and organizational type. As a result he has emerged as one of the leading international figures who is concerned with scholarly research on military institutions and the nation state.

Three elements characterize his approach. First, his orientation to the subject matter of military institutions combines historical analysis with an analytic sociological framework. He starts with the contributions of Max Weber which he enriches by contemporary organization theory. His analytic framework is explicated by the most exacting empirical research—based both on historical documentation and current field research. If there is a "European" mode and an "American" mode of sociological endeavor, Jacques van Doorn has effectively fused both.

Second, for him, the study of military institutions is at the heart of the analysis of macrosociology—the analysis of the nation state. His interests encompass both the emergence of the nation state in Western Europe and the contemporary transformation of military institutions which nuclear weapons and the decline of conscription are accomplishing. In the recent past, sociologists have been prepared to analyze the role of the military in the emergence of nationalism in Latin America, and in the "new nations" of Africa, the Middle East, and Asia. However, these same sociologists have tended to describe the emergence of the industrialized nation states of Western Europe including the United States, mainly in terms of political and economic change, that is, without adequate reference to the consequences of military institutions. Jacques van Doorn's writings make the continuation of this intellectual distortion impossible. Nationalism and national development in the Western nation state must also be analyzed in terms of the impact of their military institutions and the patterns of warmaking if the particular conditions which permitted the development of civilian control and competitive parliamentary institutions in the West are to be understood adequately.

Third, he is concerned with the interplay between systematic propositions and empirical data. As a result his approach encompasses the micro as well as the macro elements of military organization. To apply organization theory to the analysis of military formations and socio-political changes requires an examination of the informal, intimate, and small group relations of an institution. The difficulties of collecting such data hardly relieve the sociologist of this obligation. Global theories of history and sociology and simplistic causal explanations do not suffice in his interpretation. He displays remarkable talent in the uncovering of evidence on the structure and operation of the smallest units of military organization. The micro level of analysis is to be found whether he is analyzing the historical introduction of new organizational procedures and discipline in the military as it became professional, or when he is reporting on field research on the excessive use of force by the Dutch army in counter-insurgency in Indonesia.

The Soldier and Social Change represents sociological analysis in the "grand manner." It encompasses the broad sweep of historical "time" from the start of the 17th century—the period of the first "rationally" planned military organization—to the contemporary epoch of the post World War II period. But Jacques van Doorn's goals are hardly that of an historical chronicle. Instead he focuses on three nodal issues which he sees as central in the process of historical change. First, is the growth and impact of professionalism in the modern—that is, the post feudal—military establishment of Western Europe.

Jacques van Doorn uses a two-fold strategy to analyze the rise and transformation of post feudal military institutions. On the one hand, his concern with the formulations of Max Weber leads him to press for a comparative analysis of industrial versus military organization. The central elements of Protestant thought which emphasized work ethic and attendant concepts of organizational discipline were to be found earlier in military institutions than in industrial organization. In fact, his historical investigation highlights the conclusion that "modern" military organization emerged at least two centuries before "modern" industrial organization. In essence, the historical perspective emphasizes the transfer of the military format into the industrial sector. However, in the contemporary period, industrial organization has become the dominant model of organization, and the military professional is under pressure to confront the imagery of industrial management. The results are new and pervasive sources of tensions and defensiveness among military professionals.

On the other hand, the van Doorn analysis examines the fusion of professionalism and bureaucratic organization. In any large scale organization strains exist between professional practice and the power relations of hierarchy. But these tensions are particularly sharp in the military, in part because the military profession is not a free profession. It can only be practised in the employ of the state. Likewise, these tensions are pronounced in the military, in part, because the goals of the military are so overriding and central that professionalism is subject to extensive political control, both in parliamentary and one party political regimes. Yet the implication of his analysis is that professional norms are essential elements in accounting for the patterns of "rationality" which are to be found in military organizations.

The second aspect of his focus is on the dilemmas and tensions which the contemporary military profession in parliamentary regimes face. Internally, there is the strain on traditional authority, and externally, there are the problematic issues of civil-military relations in the search for a new basis for civilian control during a period in which the politico-military goals of the armed forces are undergoing change. In dealing with the internal aspect of the contemporary transformation of the armed forces, his thrust is to speak of the crisis of legitimacy—a term which is resisted and rejected by the professional officer. He points to the special dilemmas of the military given its increasing technological base, and to the convergence in authority problems of the military with other central institutional sectors of an advanced industrial society. The model which he sees as emerging is some form of "reprofessionalization" in which the notion of the citizen soldier weakens and new cadres of military emerge with more distinct boundaries from civilian society.

The issue of authority is external as well—that is, it involves civil-military relations and new elements of civilian control. Jacques van Doorn confronts the formulations of Samuel Huntington. His comparative analysis augments the standard practice of contrasting the industrialized West with the developing nations. He effectively includes the available data on the one party states of the USSR and Eastern Europe. The result is new evidence to reject Samuel Huntington's thesis that military professionalism makes for political neutrality; that is, if new evidence is required. Likewise, his conclusions call into question the argument that political culture as posited by Samuel Finer—is the central explanation of civilian control—including its forms in the one party states. For van Doorn, instead civilian control rests on mechanisms of organizational control, and on value systems which emphasize the detachment of the professional military from the political process. The term "detachment" hardly means social isolation. It rather implies the development of a set of norms which regulate the professional military so that they understand the basic logic of their political regime.

Third, Jacques van Doorn explores the relation of the military establishments of Western Europe to their counterpart elements in the colonial scheme, both historical and in the final decline of Western colonialism. The issue of center and periphery is here at work. In other words, it is impossible to analyze Western military establishments without examining their impact on colonialism and in turn the final impact of the end of colonialism on the Western military. In order to probe the linkages between the military institutions at the center—in the European metropole—and those in the colonial periphery, he examines the case of the Dutch involvement in Indonesia. This case parallels the experience of France (and by analogy that of the United States in South Vietnam), rather than that of the withdrawal from the Empire of the British military. His analysis focuses on the emergence of the colonial army as a differentiated institution from the central home establishment and on its highly selective social basis of recruitment in the indigenous population. Such a military institution has a specialized political basis in the politically conservative elements at home although it is able to invoke the symbolism of nationalism and patriotism. The central issue of the sociology of post World War II colonial intervention deals not only with the forms of military operations which were supposed to defeat the nationalist forces; van Doorn also isolated the institutional elements which led both the political and military leaders to misjudge the political context in which they were operating.

He also presents a remarkable study based on operational records of the field conditions which contributed to the military's resort to excessive violence—and emergence of atrocities—and the resulting point of no return. The end of colonial involvement of the armies of Western Europe brings with it the preconditions for the new military professional which must deal with the ambiguities of a new domestic internal politics and the strategy of "no" strategy—namely that of deterrence.

The Inter-University Seminar on Armed Forces and Society is pleased to sponsor the publication of these penetrating essays. Jacques van Doorn is not only a research scholar of real competence, but he has acted as a leader in international collaboration in the study of militarism and civil-military relations. For almost a decade he has been a central figure in the work of the Research Committee on Armed Forces and Society of the International Sociological Association. In no small measure, he has been responsible for the growth of this research group. He has served as editor of the proceedings of its various international Congresses held at Evian, France (1966), London (1968), Varna, Bulgaria (1970) and more currently Toronto (1974).* He has pressed for effective scholarly standards and resisted the intrusion of political, ideological and

---

*Jacques van Doorn (ed.), *Armed Forces and Society* (The Hague: Mouton, 1968).

Jacques van Doorn (ed.), *Military Profession and Military Regimes* (The Hague: Mouton, 1969).

Morris Janowitz and Jacques van Doorn (eds.), *On Military Intervention, On Military Ideology* (Rotterdam: University of Rotterdam Press, 1971).

representational elements into the comparative analysis of military institutions. There can be no truly international and comparative research without the opportunity for face-to-face contact among scholars from different national settings; and Jacques van Doorn has contributed to the emergence and persistence of meaningful contacts across national boundaries.

I take the opportunity of this preface to stress my deep appreciation for his colleagueship which for many years has been a source of great satisfaction and support to me in a period in which scholarly research into military institutions, war, revolutions and peace keeping had to face extensive institutional and ideological resistance in sociological circles. But I believe that we have made some progress in overcoming these barriers although much remains to be accomplished.

Morris Janowitz
The University of Chicago
Near South Side
Chicago, Illinois
September, 1974

Part One

THE EMERGENCE

OF THE

MODERN MILITARY

Chapter 1

THE GENESIS OF MILITARY AND INDUSTRIAL ORGANIZATION

INTRODUCTION

*L*arge organizations are human creations of the highest order. They constitute the living example that man is able not only to adequately exploit natural resources but also to efficiently utilize the source of power that develops where many cooperate simultaneously to achieve a common goal. By adapting himself to the structures imposed by the desire for efficiency man can realize projects which are unattainable for each separate individual. What he loses in personal liberty by participating in the collective effort, he regains by sharing in the collective results.

History shows how difficult it is to organize on a grand scale. In the past, the truly successful, reasonably adequately functioning organizations constituted exceptions to the rule that organized co-operation can slip as easily into conflict and anarchy as it can degenerate into a reign of terror by the few over the many. Only in recent times has the awareness grown that such danger can be avoided by recognizing the three-fold character of each organization: i.e. its character as a rational construction, as a unit of cooperation and as a social institution.

An organization is a rational construction to the extent that it is an instrument: that is to say, insofar as its basic principles and working procedures flow directly from its purpose. An organization has such purposefulness as its essence or, to put it more strongly, as a design it can, in its main traits and in its details, only be understood in terms of its purpose.[1]

At the same time, however, an organization constitutes a grouping, a being-together and being-united of a number of people who do not only escape from the organizational design in the way that people escape from all constructions, but who also deviate from the scheme time and again because they are inclined to interpret their own function in the organization in their own way, on the basis of their own personality, social origin and educational level, economic interest, political convictions and ideological views.

Finally, an organization as a social institution constitutes the reflection of a certain social order, a certain technological level and a certain culture. Those people who consider the testimony of history as being too far removed to provide accurate insight, can still observe the results of the introduction into non-Western regions of such Western organizational forms as public services, military formations, and school systems, not to speak of the optimistic export of complete steel industries and blast-furnaces.

It is necessary, because of this threefold character of organization—construction, grouping and institution—to look at usual studies of the organization phenomenon with a critical eye. In the past what was presented as organizational theory originated too often from the one-sided viewpoint of construction: this is understandable when we look at the professional background of many of these theorists—engineers—and at the time and place of origin of the theory—viz. late nineteenth century industry. On the other hand, in the contributions from the social sciences side there was a lack of understanding of the organization as a goal-oriented system and social theorists limited themselves to pointing to deviant behavior— the notorious "informal organization"—or to talking about adaptation difficulties.

The consequence of all this was that, on the one hand, people believed somewhat too readily in the omni-applicability of a number of nicely-constructed organizational principles, whereas, on the other hand, great efforts were made to show that human groups and social institutions differ in structure and function to such an extent that each attempt to compare them from the point of view of organization and organizability must *a priori* be deemed fruitless.[2]

Happily, this situation has been changing rapidly in the last years. There is at present a continuous flow of publications, demonstrating determined efforts to analyze very different kinds of organizations and trace common traits in order to arrive at a realistic, "renovated" theory of organizations.

Yet it is a pity that, thus far, little effort has been made to systematically compare organizations different in purpose and function which come from clearly distinct social sectors. Comparative studies of this kind could amount to a decisive step by casting aside the text-book atmosphere of organization principles, on the one hand, and the comprehensive organization monographs, on the other, in order to lay the foundations for a general empirical science of organization.

The best thing to do in this case is to join effort to argument and set ourselves on a path which thus far has been rarely trodden, and submit military and industrial organizations to comparative "research-in-outline."

At first sight it seems fully comprehensible that very little has been done in the field of comparative studies of army and industry.[3] What, indeed, is the similarity between an infantry combat unit and the crew of a steel mill; between a soap factory and a tank batallion; between cavalry officers and sales managers? This way of putting the question is, however, based on the tendency to set store to external and fortuitous things. The question which should be asked is of an analytical nature. Taking our point of departure from the fact that armies as well as industries are evidently organizations, that is to say, social structures in which members' activities are fixated into functions coordinated in relation to a certain goal[4]—taking this point of departure we can then ask to what extent, in what way, and under which conditions are military and industrial efforts in fact organized?

For discussion purposes, this general question can be split into three parts. Firstly, it is worthwhile to investigate the pattern of early organization; secondly, how it is that in both sectors such massive formal organizations have come about; thirdly, we need to compare some stages of development, distinguished according to the role that basic technical factors have played in them.

THE EARLY PATTERN OF ORGANIZATION

The first question, i.e., the genesis of military and industrial organization, confronts us, in the nature of the case, with historical material but is not intended in an historical sense. The fact that the earliest rationally-planned forms of military organization had already acquired their shape in the Western Europe of around 1600, while those in the industrial sector only formed during the nineteenth century, certainly constitutes a curious fact[5] but does not concern us here. Our problem is: how have people solved the problem, when first confronted with it, of controlling, manipulating and motivating great numbers of individuals brought together to achieve a common goal?

Speaking quite generally, people first solved this difficulty by adopting ready-made solutions. So, as regards this initial period, we can hardly speak of "new construction", only of a "supra-structure" superimposed on already existent structures, of auxiliary constructions and temporary measures.

The first thing present was the motivation to achieve good results. Would it be too risky to assume that, after the Middle Ages, the first regular military organizations benefited from what was left of the traditions of knightly warfare, especially as far as mental attitudes were concerned?[6] Wouldn't, in the same way, the start of the industrial revolution have been facilitated by the presence of a tradesman-like ethic of labour, now at the service of factory production?

The relation between puritanism and the ethics of duty posited by Weber appears in a new light, if one realizes that not only the beginnings of modern capitalism but also those of the modern army —with its emphasis on duty, discipline, self-sacrifice and regularity —are to be found in Protestant countries: the Dutch Republic, England (under Cromwell), Sweden, and later, Prussia. Speier comments in this connection: "the rise of modern military discipline in the sixteenth century was so closely related to Protestant religious beliefs that the new discipline became known in Europe as the Protestant discipline."[7]

It is, in any case, certain that a strong appeal had to be made to existing professional knowledge and experience. Special training was still lacking: the foot soldier and trooper brought in his self-acquired skills—also his own weapons—and his usefulness increased with his age, via which he became a trained man.[8] In much the same way, new industry must have drawn on the skills of the tradesman, leaving the rest to experience acquired on the job. This could, indeed, be sometimes a very rational procedure. There were of old small units which aimed at the development of skills and which reflected in their hierarchical structure differences in capacity and seniority. It is well-known that in nineteenth century factories the master-apprentice relation was still accepted and was "built into" the larger system in such a way that the specific functions of the foreman as regards placement, training and payment of personnel were retained.[9]

In such a set-up, the factory foreman of today—having as a level a supervisory function in the line hierarchy—was still unknown, just as the modern non-com. officer did not occur in the mercenary armies of the sixteenth century. The original "company" had the traits of a guild, the members of which chose their own foreman; this was a right they retained when they were later incorporated into bigger military formations: the lower cadre was appointed from and by the ranks.[10]

In the cavalry one then sees small, fairly autonomous fighting units, consisting of the traditional nobly-born horseman and his retinue, now, by way of compromise, incorporated into a cavalry corps.[11]

However, such use of existing organizational forms was insufficient and therefore additional organizational formulae became necessary. In the case of both army and industry, the solution was sought in the putting-out of substantial tasks, including the organization these involved.

In the sixteenth century people were indeed able to muster an army consisting of cavalry and infantry, but all kinds of tasks which are now allocated to the artillery and engineering corps were then put out to civilian entrepreneurs, e.g., the construction of entrenchment works, of galleries for canal causeways and mines, and the erection of gun positions. As a matter of fact, the oldest organizations in the field of artillery were guilds and consisted of civilians.[12]

Even more important was the fact that people were sometimes

not even able to take care of the recruitment and organization of personnel and had to rely on middlemen for this: the recruiting sergeant and the subcontractor are similar figures from the same early-organizational stage. In much the same way, personnel is still separately provided for each job by labor brokers and subcontractors in some branches of industry, e.g., the big ports,[13]—a practice which was fairly general during the Industrial Revolution in other branches as well[14] (the sixteenth century army was recruited for each campaign via intermediaries in the service of a prince or state).[15]

The principal, who was also the future pay-lord, then gave an officer of good reputation a "commission" ("Bestallung") as commander. The strength of the troops, payment and other conditions of delivery were stipulated in a contract. The commander, in his turn, contacted a number of officers who, in the function of captain, had to form a company; the place of mustering and the date on which the regiment would be formed were also agreed. The captains again sent recruiting agents to the main population centers, and after a certain time the unit required would assemble at the mustering place, where it would be formed officially and with the necessary ritual, and hence the army became at the pay-lord's disposal.[16]

Max Weber speaks rightly here of a "capitalistic provision and organization of the army"[17] and within the framework of the evolution of a capitalistic economy, it is a salient fact that with the expansion of the administrative and organizational capacities of the government at least a part of the production apparatus has followed the armed forces on their road to nationalization. Sixteenth century government formation of an army via contractors was not inspired by basic principle but by reasons of a technical-organizational character: it could not master such a task itself.[18]

That the military as well as the industrial organization finally had to abandon these compromise constructions, can be explained from the growing disfunctional character of such forms.

On the one hand, the army as well as industry had to deal with a stream of personnel having no useful traditions, which entailed increasing necessity to create in their own way a cooperative structure from this material. On the other hand, a lot of tradition only constituted an inconvenience: after all, knightly as well as craft individualism is, in the last analysis, incompatible with the requirements of a stringently goal-oriented organization.[19] Wherever a standing apparatus is required, either for guarding frontiers or for continuous production, the whole system of subcontractors constitutes an absurdity because it provides great possibilities for chicanery and sabotage.

This is not to say however that certain traits of "military capitalism" have not had a long existence, e.g., in France, and in several German states until right into the eighteenth century. Recruitment practices gave rise to great scandals, and some German princes indulged in the choice practice of selling their subjects as soldiers to be used in British colonial expeditions.[20] The recruitment methods of the French Foreign Legion, moreover, are of a far more recent date.

THE EMERGENCE OF FORMAL ORGANIZATION

It is very interesting to observe that the more rational organization of the army—which began in several countries, but in the Dutch Republic in particular, around 1600—and, three centuries later, of industry, show similar characteristics which sometimes agree even in detail. In both cases the point of departure was the promotion of effectivity, by analyzing systematically and precisely the existing organization and testing this on the final goals of the system: productivity, respectability, battle-power.

The similarity in approach is immediately obvious, and can be best demonstrated by an analysis of the procedures of such seemingly incomparable figures as Maurice of Orange, the founder of the the "classical" military organization, and the American engineer Taylor, the man of "scientific management." With both persons one is struck by the solid knowledge of the practice of their trade, their sharp analytical powers and a desire for experiment which was supported by a firm belief in the organizability and manipulability of human behaviour.[21]

But their similarity is also striking as far as their preoccupation with detail is concerned. The thing Taylor and his followers aimed at and effectuated, i.e., the decomposition of human labor into its components of movement in order to arrive, by its reconstruction, at the most efficient performance, had already been applied by Maurice three centuries earlier to the handling of weapons. In this fashion the handship of the musket was broken down into a prescribed series of 43 separate movements, and the use of the pike into 23, which had to be practised one by one, individually at first and then in formation.[22]

The reorganization of army and industry went further, of course, than this. In agreement with the essence of organisation, activities were mainly deployed in two directions: the hierarchical structure was made more rigid and performance was perfectionized.

To begin with, a lot was to happen with the hierarchy. The most characteristic trait of the development of military organization is the gradual disappearance of the identity between the dichotomies of nobility/commoner and officer/ranks: the organizational criterion takes the place of status distinctions.[23] This shift is also expressed in the punishments provided by military law: the old difference between nobility and commoners disappears and, in its place, a distinction according to military rank is introduced.[24] The nobility retains an important share of the leading positions, to be sure, but it evolves from being a privileged social elite to being an upper cadre in the army organization.

The noble officer was also divested of his personal or hired retinue: "the ordinances concerning the infantry are directed against disobedience and mutiny, those concerning the cavalry against entrepreneurship".[25]

The comparison between this development in military organization and the gradual decline of owners' rights in the industrial enterprise seems more forced than it really is. In the same way as the nobility had at their disposal a privilege of birth, the son of the entrepreneur possessed a privilege-without-effort; the shift from noble to military official is, just as that from owner to salaried manager, a shift from ascribed status to achieved status.[26] One could also say that in both sectors an increasing professionalization of top sectors is to be observed: an evolution from status and class privilege to profession.

One should not conclude from the above that this development took place exponentially. One gains the strong impression that sixteenth and seventeenth century armies offered a fair number of possibilities for promotion: "the new armies, in fact, served as the social escalators of the age."[27] But the promotion of commoner officers into nobility ranks also points to the existing tendency to maintain homogeneity and preserve the caste of officers.[28]

In any case, the profession of military officer was in France in the eighteenth century and in Germany until well into the nineteenth century, mainly, an affair of the nobility. Following the democratization which took place during and after the French Revolution, counter-currents could be observed in France in the second half of the last century.[29] Even in Holland, a bourgeois country par excellence, the military top-group retained for a long time a strong aristocratic flavoring. In 1872, 22% of army generals and colonels were of noble origin, in 1931 12%, and in 1950 0%.[30]

Just as the inheritance of profession guarantees a certain exclusiveness in the organizational top group of the forces, the inheritance of property contributes to the fact that industrial leaders remain in a milieu that is to some extent insulated. A study of the American business elite on type of career discloses, for instance, the fact that the number of salaried managers, in percentage terms, has risen continuously over the last one and a half centuries, to be sure, but that the number of heirs in the top group has relatively increased. Until the middle of the last century the percentage of heirs among big entrepreneurs remained at about 20%, after that at about 35%. The percentage of typical "managers", however, increased in this period from 10-20% to almost 50%.[31]

It is interesting to compare this result with the fact that among commissioned officers in the US army (infantry), the percentage of officers' sons rose from 4% in 1910, to 23% in 1935. With the growth in the army and the recruitment procedure during and after the Second World War, this percentage decreased sharply to 11% in 1950.[32]

Much more striking is the phenomenon in the French army, where "self-recruitment" has increased sharply over the last few decades. In 1960, no less than 44% of the students at military academies came from a military milieu; in 30% of these cases, the father was a commissioned officer, in 14% a non-commissioned officer.[33]

In Holland, around 1950, this same figure was 22% for students of the Royal Military Academy; for students of the Naval Academy in the fifties 30%.[34]

In trade and industry, as well as in the armed forces, there are certain sectors which show a much more pronounced succession from within their own milieu than outside it. To continue with some Dutch figures: among army officers in 1960 (of the rank of captain and higher), the percentage of those of noble origin in the cavalry was almost 10% of the total figure, in the infantry not even 1%.[35] Research into the top management of several hundreds of big firms in Holland showed that in the textile industry in almost 57% of all cases the son succeeded the father in his directorship, as compared with a percentage of 34.7 for all firms together.[36]

If with professionalization a bureaucratization begins in both industry and the forces, then in the forces this happens far earlier and is far more progressed than in trade and industry. This difference is related, to an important extent, to the traditionally much greater size of the forces. Only contemporary big business constitutes a fit object of comparison and it is exactly here indeed, that a certain bureaucratization is further progressed.

Yet here too the standardization of functions is still far less than it is in the forces, because these are set up along broad lines which follow one pattern as appears from a comparison of both sectors: "rapid succession, typical of highly bureaucratic systems, characterized the military installation to a much greater extent than it did the business firm".[37]

This development can be ascribed inter alia, in the army as well as in trade and industry, to a shift in functional emphasis from the bottom of the organization to the top. In the same way as Maurice of Orange tripled the number of officers per company, so Taylor also drastically expanded the number of cadre per work group.[38] The task of management becomes heavier to the extent that the initiative is taken out of the hands of subordinates.

This latter fact leads us to the consequences of reorganization at the shop floor level. I have already pointed to the similarity in precise task analysis for soldier and laborer and, arising from this, to the possibility for precise instruction and training. The limitations on personal initiative, however, went even further than this. Discipline, precision, order and cleanliness become the keywords. The ideal is an organization in which all parts consist of perfectly functioning people who subordinate themselves totally to the common goal. Seen in this way, Maurice of Orange's army can be characterized (via a term pertaining to the industrial sphere) as a manufacture-organization, because the laborers and their tools—the soldiers and their weapons—constitute the composite elements.[39] In the same sense, Frederick the Great was as much a perfectionist as Taylor: they both perfectionized to the extreme the labor-intensive organization.

The similarity is not fortuitous. Both were confronted with the problem of how a mass of badly trained, moderately motivated individuals, who were also cut off from their old social milieu, could be welded into goal-attainment organization. Both had the proletariat as a recruiting pool, and in spite of all differences which can undoubtedly be pointed out, their mechanistic image of man was also a product of the circumstances in which they had to work.[40]

When even the proletariat refused to be recruited, direct force was used instead. It is well-known that early capitalistic enterprises profited greatly from the population available in poorhouses and orphanages, and that the English navy was for a long time manned mainly via the activities of the press gang.[41] In the eighteenth century these forms of compulsion often coincided. Soldiers, expensively maintained in peace-time, were often made temporarily productive in workshops: "military barracks in Austria and Prussia were veritable spinning mills."[42]

In this kind of scheme personal relations, let alone paternalistic ones, played far less of a role than had formerly been the case. The hierarchy became more rigid and functional. Old democratic rights, such as the selection of lower cadre by the ranks, disappeared in the course of the seventeenth century.[43] In much the same way, the relation between master and apprentice melts away. The middle-man becomes foreman, just as the leader of mercenaries becomes a non-commissioned officer, a strictly hierarchical figure, incorporated into the formal organization.[44]

Since then, the foreman as well as the non-commissioned officer has provided the standard example of "the man with a role conflict", placed as he is between the incompatible expectations of his superiors and his subordinates, too near the lower layer to be independent from his men, too clearly a part of the line hierarchy not to "toe the line." The foreman has been called a "master and victim of double talk"—

research shows that the non-commissioned officer also has a claim to this description.[45]

The final result, in the army as well as in trade and industry, is a form of organization primarily directed to the, as far as possible, total use of a with difficulty manipulable human effort. This organization exists thanks to the presence of a powerless proletariat and it believes in the superior insight of a strongly dominating elite of leaders. It does not have to reckon with technical elements of any significance and hence can totally direct itself to the exploitation of human capacities.

According to the ideology of organization, a man is only capable of purposive action when he is told continuously and precisely what to do and how to do it. This form of control is based on the conviction that, in the last analysis, the worker does not want to work and the soldier does not want to fight: they have to be induced to do so by forceful measures.

It is not difficult to similarly apply the concepts of "alienation" and "Verdinglichung", used so often to characterize the position of the nineteenth century industrial proletariat, to the professional soldier of the old army. Between their role in the organization and their place in society existed a direct correlation; as proletarians—without their own weapons and tools, without specific capacities or education—they had to be satisfied with what they were ordered to do or what was shifted on to them.

THE TECHNICAL REVOLUTION

The industrial as well as the military revolution has had a double face. On the one hand, labor was more systematically used, on the other hand machines were introduced. To put it briefly, in addition to task distribution and task organization, task replacement was also applied.

In both cases the magnification of effect was sought. In the one case this was attained by the efficient organization of direct human effort into a group relation; in the other by replacing the human being by a far more powerful technical capacity. The energy which is compressed in a gun or in a rolling-machine, exceeds human capacities as much as does the speed of machine gun or punching machine.

The military as well as the industrial revolutions made their spectacular leap forward in the first place by a more efficient and concentrated organization of human effort, not by mechanization. The artillery, as well as mechanized industry, have for a long time played only a modest role in the magnification of military combat power and productivity respectively, however spectacular their appearance has been.[46]

What is conspicuous in all this is the continued existence of trade-like forms of organization, in the army as well as in industry. Knowledge and skills of the trade were maintained until a relatively short time ago in, for example, the glass industry, in blast furnaces and steel mills.[47] Artillerymen also continued to work in the style of tradesmen: people were trained as apprentices in using cannon and required a master's certificate. For a long time they remained organized as a guild.[48]

For the rest, the artillerymen and military engineers, often commoners or of common origin, enjoyed little prestige in military circles. Even in the seventeenth century the artillery was still not regarded as an organizationally distinct part of the services.[49] The military engineer came even far further behind. Though the German Navy abandoned sailing around 1850, it was only in 1870 that the first very modest possibility was created for technicians to obtain a military service rank. The *"Machinemann"* was actually not counted as being a soldier. Even the management of the naval ship-yards remained in the hands of inexpert naval officers.[50]

Gradually, however, mechanization grew in significance, by which process industry came abreast, in the course of the nineteenth century, with the military apparatus, then overtook it and even remained ahead for a considerable period of time. To put it very schematically: industry copied the organization of labor from the army, and then further developed this technique on its own, though it was stimulated in all this by the forces and especially by the old weapons industry.

It is necessary now to give a comparative analysis of types of organization in the present, very mechanized, mode of production and style of warfare. What are the consequences for the management and execution of tasks in those organizations in which human energy is oriented mainly towards guiding, controlling and servicing activities in connection with machines and installation?

Firstly, as far as the managing elite in both organizations is concerned, one cannot say that the technician has forced out the old types of leadership. The entrepreneur and the strategist are still in the first place figures who have the task of making an organization operate in a field of action, in as efficient a way as possible, whether this field is constituted by a market or by a war.

But, though we can by no means speak of a technocracy, it remains true that specialist technicians now occupy a place in top groups to a far greater extent than was formerly the case. The engineer-officer can now become a chief-of-staff, the engineer a president-director, and the technician has also made his debut into the cadres surrounding these functions.[51]

The significance of engineering (and the technical sciences) is further underlined by the fact that in both sectors the engineer was the first academic to be taken up in great numbers into the apparatus. It even used to be the case that a civil engineer was dependent for his training on military schools of engineering (the famous French Ecole Polytechnique, and the predecessor of the present Dutch Military Academy, viz., the School of Artillery and Engineering in Delft, founded in 1814, where those specializing in hydraulic engineering were also trained).[52]

The activities entailed in leadership have certainly become much heavier through the growing complexity of organization and the mechanization of activities. The time that an officer could leave his troops to a sergeant-major and the factory owner could rely entirely on a foreman has passed. The coordination of technical and administrative, personnel and organization functions has become a complicated task. Training, maintenance research and development require continuous attention.

The growing burden of the managerial task led to a demand for schooling in which the forces took the lead in the previous century, a demand trade and industry are now following, though sometimes rather hesitantly. The question of explaining the relatively early rise of the military academy and the relatively late interest for the "business school" I will leave aside here;[53] it is certain that in both milieus a clear resistance against higher schooling existed and—certainly as

far as in several European countries trade and industry is concerned
—still exists. The British Naval Academy, founded in 1733, met with
little approbation: "What's the use of book-learning to sea-officers
anyway?" One century later the British Army similarly displayed a
total lack of interest in the Royal Military College, until the catastrophe of the Crimean War revealed the incompetence of its military
leaders. The judgement of older Dutch officers, "that Breda produced
scholars but no soldiers," when the Royal Dutch Military Academy
was founded, is of the same ilk. In the same way as they, together
with the German cavalry officers of the previous century, maintained
that one could be an officer by birth and talents, so we still encounter
the belief in the businessman who is born, not made.[54]

One can push this analogy further and elaborate on it to form a
typology of entrepreneurs and officers.

The paternalistic figure for instance: the employer in the style
of Robert Owen, who surrounds "his" people with plenty of care but
therefore demands, at the same time, complete obedience;[55] the officer who, like Napoleon, calls his soldiers *"mes enfants"* or who, like
the Prussian Junkers of the nineteenth century regard their company
as a kind of family, in which the officer rules as a *pater familias*.[56]

Another type, represented in industry as the "social entrepreneur," is a figure similar to that discussed in German military
circles shortly after 1900, viz.: the "social officer", an attempt to
respond to the challenge of social democracy by the creation of a new
type of officer.[57]

The growing technification and complicatedness is comple-
mented by the very strong expansion of middle cadre and staff functions. Headquarters both in business and armed forces have expanded simultaneously and it appears that the number of "direct"
functions, be they in the front or in the production-line, will shrink
to a minority. For both types of organization, the number of derived
functions has increased enormously and is still increasing. The
phenomenon of the middle-level employee in trade and industry is
manifested in the forces in a totally similar way.

In the American army of sixty years ago, for instance, more than
90% of the personnel had typically military tasks, as compared to
not even 30% now. The percentage of administrative personnel increased in that same period from less than 1% to more than 17%.[58]

Over the same period the percentage of administrative employees in American industry increased from almost 8% to more than 20%, thus reflecting a similar tendency.[59] Comparable data are available for other countries.

This development has led to the disappearance of the old pyramidal personnel structure of the organization, with a great mass of unskilled labor at the base and a gradually narrowing superstructure of more demanding functions. It is already the case that the lowest functions in industry, comparatively, are no longer the most numerous, just as during the Second World War the number of privates in the American army was considerably smaller than the number of "privates first class" and hardly exceeded the number of corporals.[60]

These figures are much more striking as far as a highly mechanized arm of the services, such as the airforce, is concerned; the figures here are comparable to those concerning the metals and optical industries. Here the "middle-layer" is even better represented than the rank and file. Rank is no longer determined by the number of subordinates, but by the technical capacities of the man concerned.[61]

In the executive functions mechanization has had as strong an influence. The old relation between the man and his equipment has been reversed. The armed man has become a manned weapon, the laborer and his tools a manned machine, and in both cases groups, teams and crews are often concerned which assist in servicing the machine or weapon.

This shift, which has been commented upon for a long time now as far as industry is concerned but which, in relation to the forces has been too little studied, has led to a fundamental change in the disposition and task performance of the executive personnel. Physical effort has been replaced by mental tension, through which an appeal is made to other human faculties. The pilot, the artillery man, and the tank crew do not have "to fight bravely," in the strict sense of the expression; in the same way, the crane operator and the rolling-machine operator do not have it as their prime obligation "to work hard." In both cases a combination of skill, attentiveness and "availability" is much more necessary. Foot-soldiers and porters belong to equally obsolete forms of military and productive effort, still, and perhaps for always, indispensable, but often highly inefficient and decreasing in quantitative importance.

Though the limitation of dirty, heavy and dangerous work as such must be called satisfactory, we have to wait and see what will be the influence on men of activities, the result of which can never be directly observed and weighed. This question, which has been put concerning administrative and industrial automation, can be put with equal justification in relation to military functions, in which the effect of effort is not only invisible but also can not be assessed. There is as little place here for the old military virtues as there is for a craftsman's in highly mechanized industry.

Not only the individual but also the small group is placed in relation to the technical process. The crew of a gun, a radar post, aeroplane, tank or submarine are connected not only by a common commander but by a common task, which can only be properly performed by a team.[62] The formation of such teams has consequently become an important task for management.

It has not been as clearly noticed that the same formations, and comparable problems, occur in industry where the crew of a rolling-machine, blast, steel or glass furnace also consists of a working team, the cohesion of which is based on a coordinated operating of the apparatus.

This functional structure of the executive level has a direct effect on hierarchical relations. A disciplinary pattern of authority is not only less possible in these groups, it is also less necessary. The relative autonomy of the technical process defines what has to be done: "this results from the mechanics of the technical installation."[63]

Future research has yet to determine whether the relative independence of such military and industrial teams has not been limited in recent times by improved methods of central process control and communication. The better a process in a blast furnace can be computed and controlled, the smaller the room for initiative of the servicing personnel, and the greater the possibility for integration in a vast production process. In the same way the former scope for initiative of the jet pilot, tank and gun crews will be limited by continuous communication with higher command posts.

For the rest, there seems to be, exactly on this point of hierarchy, a difference in development between industry and infantry. In both sectors, external compulsion from above is, to be sure, no longer very efficient, but whereas the grip on subordinate employees in trade and industry is increasing all the time via more and more careful programming, modern warfare enforces on the military fighting unit a high degree of initiative and improvization, which constitutes a really urgent problem for the conventional pattern of authority.

One thing is certain, viz., that the mass character of manufacturing and of the old army has disappeared. Modern industry, just as the modern military organization, is a very complicated and highly structured goal-oriented system in which there is no place for massive concentrations. The depopulation of the modern battlefield finds its parallel in the depopulation of the shop floor in highly mechanized industry. The mass is in this sense contrary to what one would have expected, *not* a modern phenomenon.

The rediscovery of the small group as an organizational unit and as the cadre of motivation for the individual man is of equal importance for both military and industrial organizations. It would be interesting to compare the experiences gained in both sectors, because it is an established fact that the small group strongly influences the productivity of the laborer as well as the combat morale of the soldier.[64]

A remarkable consequence of the structure of such mighty technical complexes as modern industry and the modern forces is, finally, the relative immobility of the system. In spite of all the built-in conversion mechanisms, the organization as such functions on the basis of a fixed technical and operational structure, embedded in an infrastructure which is equally immobile.

Just as the strategist, the entrepreneur has lost his character as speculator and adventurer. He has, to formulate it somewhat gloomily, become the prisoner of his own apparatus. To put it in a more neutral way: he has gradually, in spite of all individual latitude, become a functionary. His personal preferences are subordinated to the functions of his organization.

With this, the basis of leadership has changed. It is characteristic for the modern industrial manager and the military commander that his authority is legitimated by his "functional value." One accepts him as the man who, by his activities, has shown and keeps showing that he can take command.

This double functionalization of leadership constitutes the end phase of an organizational development which began at the base and gradually embraced more and more members of the organization. Taken in this sense, modern military and industrial organization appears to be characteristic for the kind of social order in which not birth, status or class membership determines function, but where functional contribution is becoming more and more the deciding criterion.

NOTES

[1] In this statement things are consciously simplified. An organization can have more than one goal and these goals can even conflict with each other; it is also evident that sometimes no clear goal exists. Yet it is correct to emphasize that, in contrast to other social groupings, formal organizations are always goal-oriented.

[2] This has been treated more extensively in J. A. A. van Doorn, *Sociologie van de organisatie* (Leyden: Stenfert Kroese, 1956), first part.

[3] I mention a few studies, only partly sociological, here: E. H. Phelps Brown, 'Morale, Military and Industrial', *Economic Journal* Vol. LIX (1949); John Robert Beishline, *Military Management for National Defense* (Englewood Cliffs, N.J.: Prentice-Hall, 1950); P. Cabernard, *Die Anordnungen als Mittel der betriebswirtschaftlichen und der militärischen Organisation* (1963); William M. Evan, 'Due Process of Law in Military and Industrial Organizations', *Administrative Science Quarterly,* Vol. VII (1962/63), 187-207; Oscar Grusky, 'The Effects of Succession: A Comparative Study of Military and Business Organization' in Morris Janowitz (ed.), *The New Military* (N.Y.: Russell Sage Foundation, 1964), 83-111. Though the title suggests otherwise, the work of T. T. Paterson, *Morale in War and Work* (1955) is entirely limited to the Royal Air Force.

[4] For an elucidation of this definition see Van Doorn, *op. cit.,* 37 ff.

[5] It is not only curious, it is important in explaining the fact that industrial organization was influenced by military organization and technique; see Waldemar Kaempffert, 'War and Technology', *The American Journal of Sociology,* Vol. XLVI (1940-41), 431 ff.

[6] Eugen van Frauenholz, *Das Heerwesen des Reiches in der Landsknechtszeit* (München, 1937), 8.

[7] Hans Speier, ' "The American Soldier" and the Sociology of Military Organization', in Robert K. Merton and Paul F. Lazarsfeld (eds.), *Continuities in Social Research: Studies in the Scope and Method of 'The American Soldier'* (Glencoe, Ill.: The Free Press, 1950), 115. Already Weber himself called Puritanism 'the father of modern military discipline.' Max Weber, 'Die protestantische Ethik und der Geist des Kapitalismus', *Die protestantische Ethik* (München und Hamburg: Siebenstern, 1965), 215.

[8] J. W. Wijn, *Het krijgswezen in den tijd van Prins Maurits* (Utrecht, 1934), 3.

[9] Data on England in the 19th century can be found in: Reinhard Bendix, *Work and Authority in Industry: Ideologies of Management in the Course of Industrialization* (New York: Wiley & Sons, 1956), 52 ff.; Neil J. Smelser, *Social Change in the Industrial Revolution* (London: Routledge & Kegan Paul, 1959), 103-105.

[10] Wijn, *op cit.,* 12; Von Frauenholz, *op. cit.,* 41. The German historian G. Droysen had already elaborated the similarity between company and guild in 1875; see Michael Roberts, *The Military Revolution 1560-1660* (Inaugural Lecture, Queen's University of Belfast, 1956. Private circulation), 22.

[11] Eugen von Frauenholz, *Das Söldnertum in der Zeit des Dreissigjährigen Krieges* (München, 1938), 12.

[12] Wijn, *op. cit.,* 3, 47 f.

25

[13]*The Dock Worker: An Analysis of Conditions of Employment in the Port of Manchester* (University of Liverpool, 1954), 58 ff.; H. J. Helle, *Die unstetig beschäftigten Hafenarbeiter in den nordwest-europäischen Häfen* (1960), 12 ff.

[14]Bendix, *op. cit.*, 53 ff.

[15]Wijn, *op. cit.*, 11 ff.; Von Frauenholz, 'Heerwesen', *op. cit.*, 46 ff.

[16]Van Doorn, *op. cit.*, 74 f.

[17]Max Weber, 'Wirtschaft und Gesellschaft', *Grundriss der Sozialökonomik,* III (Tübingen: Mohr/Paul Siebeck, (1925, 2nd ed.), 665: 'die privatkapitalistische Heeresbeschaffung und—Verwaltung.'

[18]Wijn, *op. cit.*, 7.

[19]Van Doorn, *op. cit.*, 83.

[20]M. Jähns, *Heeresverfassung und Völkerleben* (Berlin, 1885, 2nd ed.), 284 ff.

[21]For Maurice see: Werner Hahlweg, *Die Heeresreform der Oranier und die Antike* (Berlin, 1941), 125 ff.

[22]Hahlweg, *op. cit.*, 32: 'Das Wesen des neuen oranischen Ausbildungssystems im Waffengebrauch bestand in der genauen, endgültigen Festlegung auch der kleinsten Handgriffe und ihrer folgerichtigen Anordnung im Sinne der Konstruktion der Waffe. Alle Handgriffe erhielten ihre eigenen Kommandoworte, gewissermassen als "Instruktionen für das Rekrutenlehrpersonal" '.

[23]Von Frauenholz, 'Söldnertum', *op. cit.*, 34 f.

[24]*Ibid.*, 11 f., 23 ff.

[25]Von Frauenholz, 'Heerwesen', *op. cit.*, 26.

[26]For the military development see Morris Janowitz, *Sociology and the Military Establishment* (New York: Russell Sage Foundation, 1965, rev. ed.), 28 ff.; a great deal has already been written about the evolution of entrepreneurship, see a.o. Bendix, *op. cit.*, 226 ff.

[27]Roberts, *op. cit.*, 24.

[28]Jähns, *op. cit.*, 287 f.; Wijn, *op. cit.*, 63.

[29]Mattei Dogan, 'Les officiers dans la carrière politique', *Revue Francaise de Sociologie,* Vol. II (1961), 91 f.; J. Meynaud, 'Les militaires et le pouvoir', *ibid.,* 83. For Germany: Karl Demeter, *Das Deutsche Offizierkorps in Gesellschaft und Staat 1650-1945* (Frankfurt am Main: Bernard & Graeffe Verlag für Heerwesen. 1962, rev. ed.), ch. 1.

[30]Jacques van Doorn, 'The Officer Corps: A Fusion of Profession and Organization', *Archives Européennes de Sociologie,* Vol. VI (1965), 275 ff.

[31]Bendix, *op. cit.*, 228 ff.

[32]Morris Janowitz, *The Professional Soldier* (Ill.: The Free Press of Glencoe, 1960), 95.

[33]Raoul Girardet (ed.), *La crise militaire francaise 1945-1962* (Paris: Armand Colin, 1964), 38-46.

[34]Van Doorn, 'The Officer Corps', *op. cit.*, 278 f.

[35]*Ibid.*, 275 f.

[36]P. Vinke, *De maatschappelijke plaats en herkomst der directeuren en commissarissen van de open en daarmede vergelijkbare besloten naamloze vennootschappen* (Leyden: Stenfert Kroese, 1961), 311.

[37]Grusky, *op. cit.*, 89, 107; cf. Bendix, *op. cit.*, 211 ff.

[38]Van Doorn, 'The Officer Corps', *op. cit.*, 266.

[39]In Marx's formulation: 'The collective labourer, formed by the combination of a number of detail labourers, is the machinery specially characteristic of the

manufacturing period,' and, elsewhere, 'the detail labourer and his implements are the simplest elements of manufacture.' Karl Marx, *Capital* (F. Engels, ed.) (London, 1957), 333, 341.

[40]Taylor certainly paid attention to the worker and tried to improve his position, but in the last analysis, his system was oriented to stimulating laborers to as great an effort as possible. For an insight into Taylorism in operation see, H. G. J. Aitken, *Taylorism at Watertown Arsenal: Scientific Management in Action 1908-1915* (1960).

[41]Michael Lewis, *A Social History of the Navy 1793-1815* (London: Allen & Unwin, 1960), 95 ff., 139.

[42]Fritz Redlich, 'Military Entrepreneurship in Central Europe 1650-1900', *Year Book 1961, American Philosophical Society* (1962), 412.

[43]Van Frauenholz, 'Heerwesen', *op. cit.*, 26; *ibid.*, Söldnertum, *op. cit.*, 11. The administration of justice by the level involved belonged to these rights, which similarly disappeared after 1600.

[44]Bendix, *op. cit.*, 213, gives a systematic comparison of the powers of the earlier subcontractor and the present-day plant foreman.

[45]F. J. Roethlisberger, 'The Foreman: Master and Victim of Double Talk', *Harvard Business Review*, Vol. XXIII (1945); Samuel A. Stouffer, a.o., *The American Soldier* (Princeton, N.J.: Princeton U.P., 1949), Vol. I, 401-410.

[46]See for the industrial revolution: Georg Jahn, 'Die Entstehung der Fabrik', *Schmollers Jahrbuch*, Vol. LXIX (1949), 225 ff.; for the military revolution: Roberts, *op. cit.*, 26 ff.

[47]See for instance the detailed study of a group of rolling-machine workers in: Heinrich Popitz, a.o., *Das Gesellschaftsbild des Arbeiters: Soziologische Untersuchungen in der Hüttenindustrie* (Tübingen, 1957), 250 ff.

[48]Wijn, *op. cit.*, 44 ff.

[49]Demeter, *op. cit.*, 14 f.; Von Frauenholz, Sölnertum, *op. cit.*, 34.

[50]E. Alboldt, *Die Tragödie der alten deutschen Marine* (1928), 16 ff.

[51]Vinke, *op. cit.*, 292. For the military technician see Janowitz, Professional Soldier, *op. cit.*, 68 ff. and Kurt Lang, 'Technology and Career Management in the Military Establishment', in Morris Janowitz (ed.), *The New Military: Changing Patterns of Organization* (N.Y.: Russell Sage Foundation, 1964), 39 ff.

[52]C. P. Brest van Kempen, *Onderwijs en opvoeding aan de Koninklijke Militaire Academie* (Breda, 1926), 213 ff.

[53]One of the main causes of the early emergence of military school may have been the relatively early professionalization and bureaucratization of the military.

[54]Lewis, *op. cit.*, 144; Brest van Kempen, *op. cit.*, 165; Demeter, *op. cit.*, ch. II.

[55]Bendix, *op. cit.*, 46 ff.

[56]Reinhard Höhn, *Die Armee als Erziehungsschule der Nation: Das Ende einer Idee* (Bad Harzburg: Verlag für Wissenschaft, Wirtschaft und Technik, 1963), 246.

[57]Höhn, *op. cit.*, 393 ff.

[58]Janowitz, 'Professional Soldier', *op. cit.*, 65.

[59]Bendix, *op. cit.*, 214; in the period from 1947 to 1959 the number of middle-level office employees in Dutch industry increased from 14% to 19% of total personnel.

[60]L. Neundörfer, *Die Angestellten: Neuer Versuch einer Standortbestimmung* (1961), 122 ff.; Stouffer, *op. cit.*, 233; Lang, *op. cit.*, 68 ff.

[61]Janowitz, 'Professional Soldier', *op. cit.*, 33, 126; Neundörfer, *op. cit.*, 126.

[62]For the composition of the personnel of a battery of heavy anti-aircraft artillery see D. N. Solomon, 'Sociological Research in a Military Organization', *The Canadian Journal of Economics and Political Science*, Vol. XX (1954), 537.

[63]Hans-Paul Bahrdt, *Industriebürokratie: Versuch einer Soziologie des industrialisierten Bürobetriebes und seiner Angestellten* (Stuttgart: Ferdinand Enke, 1958), 29: 'Es gibt kaum noch einen Spielraum für "Anweisungen". Was zu tun ist, weiss der Arbeiter selbst, es ergibt sich aus den Gesetzlichkeiten der technischen Anlage.'

[64]As far as this is concerned, the Hawthorne inquiry had the same shock effect on industrial sociology as the studies of Stouffer and his collaborators had on military sociology.

Chapter 2

THE OFFICER CORPS:
A FUSION OF PROFESSION AND ORGANIZATION

INTRODUCTION

*I*n modern societies profession and formal organization are the most important institutional patterns controlling occupational and administrative decisions and actions. They have many characteristics in common. To use Parsons' pattern variables: in both cases we find universal standards, specificity of expertness, and affective neutrality.[1] Bureaucratic as well as professional authority is based on special knowledge and skill (*Fachwissen*) and may be characterized as functional authority.[2] Both professional and bureaucratic status are achieved, not ascribed positions.

The differences between the two patterns are, however, equally important. The professional man has a commitment to his vocation. This vocation is generally aimed at the solution of problems which are highly relevant to the central values of society, such as justice, health, and security. Bureaucrats *may* be characterized by this value-orientation, but often they occupy themselves simply with the relation between ends and means, this being the decisive working principle of many so-called instrumental organizations.

The orientation towards central societal values has led to an often formal emphasis on the social responsibility of the professional, resulting in licensure or certification, and in a code of ethics. A formal organization lacks these characteristics.

The most important difference between the professional man and the bureaucrat, however, is their distinctive frame of reference.[3]

The loyalty of the professional man is directed at his profession: his loyalty to the employing organization is low. He takes his standards and norms from the professional community, and he tries to protect these from interference by managers and administrators. His performance as a professional can only be validated by colleagues, not by his superiors and still less by laymen.

Connected with this is the "horizontal" structure of the profession, which is composed of equals, contrasting with the explicitly hierarchical structure of the formal organization.

Both patterns, especially during the last decade, tend to integrate more and more. On the one hand, the professions have often acquired an organizational apparatus, or they have been included in agencies, laboratories, public services, companies and schools. "An increasing percentage of professionals work in complex organizations (scientists, engineers, teachers, architects, even lawyers and physicians). These organizations develop their own controls; bosses, not colleagues, rule—or at minimum, power—is split among managers, professional experts, and lay boards of directors."[4]

On the other hand, the organization of the professions is matched by a professionalization of salaried specialists and managers. A number of complex organizations show a tendency to professionalization of the top. This tendency may be found most strikingly in industrial management, but also in other occupational groups, such as social workers, psychologists and sociologists.

The progressive integration of profession and organization has not failed to attract the attention of social research and theory. In a number of studies the possibilities and difficulties of this fusion have been investigated. Conflicts easily arise, and where the "interlocking controls" of professions and organizations clash, the professional seems to be the weaker partner.[5]

It is remarkable that the military profession is seldom or never mentioned in these studies. Sometimes the professional soldier is not mentioned at all, evidently because his calling is not regarded as a profession. Sometimes he is mentioned in passing, but his position is not further discussed.[6]

This may possibly be explained by referring to the relation of the military, including the officer, to his organization. He is clearly a part of the army and his loyalty to the armed forces is always high.

His organization, moreover, is not horizontally, but extremely vertically structured. Hierarchy is the backbone of all military performance, of all rights and duties, and of the entire process of personnel allocation. It is made visible in uniforms, badges and titles.

Yet the leaders of the modern armed forces, i.e., the commissioned officers, are unmistakably professional men. Their role comprises the elements of specialized expertise and competence, public responsibility, formal licence (the commission), corporateness, and a usually strong social isolation in a professional community.[7]

Seen in this light, the officer corps is an excellent and possibly unique example of the integration of profession and organization, and, moreover, with a history long enough to permit complete observation of the process of fusion.

The combination of the two structural patterns and its consequences have been noticed earlier. "Officership is a public bureaucratized profession," Huntington writes, "the officer corps is both a bureaucratic profession and a bureaucratic organization."[8] In the case of conflict an institutional solution is ready at hand: "the priority of the hierarchy of rank over the hierarchy of office." This does not abolish the tension between military obedience and professional competence, but regulates it.[9]

So far, we have assumed the fusion of profession and organization, but we have not analyzed the process, and still less undertaken to explain it. Yet such an explanation would be of the utmost importance in this discussion on recent developments of the armed forces, and developments to be expected in the future.

As we have seen, the integration of profession and organization is a very general phenomenon. We encounter here some of the basic processes in all social institutions. A better insight into the process of fusion, as shown by the armed forces, could give a better understanding of the possible combination of relevant functional requirements, as professional autonomy and organizational effectiveness. It is with this objective that we investigate the development and the tensions of the process of military organization and professionalization.

It goes without saying that our problem is far too complicated and too extensive to be treated adequately within this short contribution. We have, therefore, tried to point out the most important variables. Materials from several historical and sociological sources have been used, especially concerning some Western European countries. Further comparative as well as historical study will be needed however to refine the hypotheses presented.

We will discuss in succession the rise of military organization, the genesis of the military profession, the form of fusion of both processes and its tensions followed by some general suggestions about the present difficulties in the military establishment.

THE RISE OF MILITARY ORGANIZATION

Formal organization is a matter of degree. In its ideal form, organization means the most efficient coordination of actions and resources with a view to attaining a specific goal. The more compelling this goal, the more the formal model will be adopted.

This means that the members of an organization will act "functionally." They abandon personal preferences and subordinate their actions to the common striving for the organization goal. Personal relations between members recede into the background: like the activities, interaction, too, becomes functional and rational.

In a large scale organization with complicated activities, the need for a division of labor and a hierarchical structure makes itself strongly felt. Members cannot fulfill all tasks, neither can they judge whether their own efforts are correctly integrated in the collective effort. Everybody assumes a special task and is given a place in a hierarchical structure. Normative controls and disciplinary sanctions keep everyone "in his place."

In this way the "modern" formal organization pattern developed: a rationally ordered structure, composed of coordinated functions, kept together by hierarchical lines, and directed from the top. In this type of "instrumental" organization the relation between means and ends forms the decisive structural principle.[10]

The so-called military revolution of the sixteenth and seventeenth centuries was first of all an organizational revolution, insofar that for the first time in Western European history a well-organized and well-disciplined large scale army was formed. "The army no longer was to be a brute mass, in the Swiss style, nor a collection of bellicose individuals, in the feudal style; it was to be an articulated organism of which each part responded to impulses from above."[11] In the course of the same process the old "company," which somewhat resembled a guild, was absorbed in the hierarchically structured formation. The lower ranks, earlier regarded as the elected representatives of the men, were incorporated in the hierarchy. The old privilege of their own administration of justice was taken from them and monopolized by their superiors.[12]

Especially the reforms of Maurice of Orange[13]—smaller size of tactical units, better discipline and drill, planned handling of arms, detailed and careful training in using arms—reduced the soldier to a condition of organizational dependency such as the industrial worker in Marx' days did not yet know.

The Maurician military "scientific management" was directed primarily at the common soldier—like Taylor predominantly occupied himself with the manual worker. This, however, at once raised the matter of the position of NCO's and subalterns. Gustavus Adolphus, king of Sweden, completed the Maurician reform by giving the lower commanders their place in the military organization. "The importance of the platoon-commander begins with Gustavus."[14]

It may be said without exaggeration that in this period the organization of military conduct was standardized for centuries to come. The adoption of uniforms, the new vocabulary of command, the training in the handling of weapons, the introduction of methods of drill, of a system of ranks and tactical units, of functional differentiation and delegation to lower commanders—all this and much more meant a series of most important organizational innovations. Although the army reform was modelled to a large extent on the Ancients it is the first large scale example in modern history of rationally planned, instrumental organization. Since then it has become a standardized pattern, and as such has been imitated again and again, in military and other institutions in Europe, and later on all over the world.[15]

The officer was scarcely involved in all this. During the military revolution the formation of an officer corps began, but for centuries the officers—at least those of the higher echelons—still acted chiefly either as mercenaries or aristocrats, or both. For the mercenary, officership was a trade; for the aristocrat, a hobby.[16]

Neither model of military leadership lent itself much to effective instrumental organization. Already in the sixteenth century there are various attempts, in Germany among others, to make the officers and the aristocratic cavalry, by means of strict Articles of War, conform better to the requirements of disciplined organization,[17] but up to the eighteenth century the structure of command in the army bears the imprint of what Max Weber has called "privatkapitalistische Heeresbeschaffung und Verwaltung."[18]

The authority of the sovereign over the professional soldiers increases, it is true, but the peculiar contractual relationship still survives. A command over a regiment or a company may be purchased; primarily, of course, by the king's favorite.[19]

The navy—at least the ships—had been traditionally "nationalized;" men-of-war unlike regiments could not be private property.[20] This, however, did not rule out the possibility of highhandedness and autonomy among commanding officers. At the time, the captain of a man-of-war was as independent in his "personnel policy"—selection, training, promotion, rewards, dismissal, his lieutenant included —as the average aristocratic army commander.[21]

The result of the early development of the modern army is a clear distinction between officers and men. The rank and file are subjected to instrumental power and domination, while officers remain relatively outside this coercive organizational control. The military revolution was an organizational revolution which left most of the officers outside the reform. Only in the nineteenth century are they more fully integrated in the formal organization.

PROFESSIONALIZATION OF THE OFFICERSHIP

Although professions cannot always be clearly distinguished from occupations, professionalization as a process can be defined rather sharply. To the extent that a profession develops or an occupation is being professionalized, the status of the expertise in question is raised, and the identification of the professional with his profession is intensified. The profession stamps its members more clearly than most occupations do. Furthermore, it will develop a form of social recognition and acceptance, and often of legal protection of the professional practice.

The two most fundamental characteristics of a profession, however, are the following: (1) a special, well-integrated body of knowledge and skill, and a set of standards and norms, handed on by means
of socialization of new members; and (2) a pronounced autonomy
of the profession, generally with legal support, repelling the interference of others in the recruitment, selection, and training of candidates, as well as in the occupational conduct of the professionals
themselves.

To reach this end, a typical sequence of events is experienced.
The first step is the emergence of a full-time occupation: amateurs
become rare. Training schools are established, and soon also professional associations to raise the quality of new and old members, and
to separate the competent from the incompetent. Finally, legal protection of the monopoly of skill (certification, license, register) is
obtained, while the professionals adopt a formal code of ethics.[22]

The development of the military profession did not follow this
relatively rectilinear model. It made several starts, each followed by
a setback, together resulting in a long and rather troubled history.
Taken as a whole, the process of professionalization in Western and
Central Europe has, in the course of the centuries, made three starts.

About 1600, at the time of the military revolution, reforms in
most countries are introduced in the armed forces, resulting in a
weakening of the distinction between noblemen and commoners,
while the dividing line between officers and men grows sharper.[23]
Relatively more commoners invade the officer-class: "the new
armies, in fact, served as the social escalators of the age."[24]

Some more or less experimental professional training is begun.
From 1616 on, several German states establish military academies
and technological progress leads to the development of a science
of war.

The nobility generally has stood up well to this challenge. The
new-born officer corps did not fall back in social status to that of the
middle class recruits, but, on the contrary, the officers of common
birth became noblemen: "an officer is a gentleman," and "das
Portepee adelt."[25]

The war academies are either short-lived or offer a general education for young noblemen, rather than professional training
(Ritterakademien, Pagerien).[26]

Meanwhile, a triple foundation has been laid for future professionalization. First, the sovereigns have monopolized control over the armed forces and formalized entry to the officer corps by means of "commission," even before training for officers becomes standardized and compulsory. Second, the military caste has inherited from the dying chivalry the international code of honor and the corporate spirit, including duelling. Third, on the fringe of the armed forces, i.e., in the artillery and the engineer corps, a really scientific training begins to take form.

In the post-Napoleonic era a new wave of radical innovation in the army, especially, furthered professionalization. The profession becomes open for persons from all social classes, even in Prussia, as proved by the famous address of August 6, 1808: "Alle bisher stattgehabten Vorzüge des Standes hören beim Militär ganz auf, und jeder ohne Rücksicht auf seine Herkunft hat gleiche Rechte."[27] The new military academies, in carrying out this program, become the decisive link between ability and profession.

Towards the middle of the nineteenth century, however, this reform, too, miscarries. The officer corps again becomes a closed group, although the social elite continues to be ousted from its domineering position, except at the top of the organization.[28]

From the third quarter of the nineteenth century on, and especially since the turn of the century, professionalization makes definite headway. Most striking is the change in institutional continuity, which used to be connected with the hereditary aristocratic origin, but has become, now, to a certain extent, a professional continuity.[29]

At the same time, during the last sixty years, the shift to middle-class origin became more and more pronounced. The old aversion to professional training—and sometimes to "Bildung" in general—has been overcome to a large degree. Now the traditional branches of the services also receive some kind of scientific training.

The military profession, however, differs from other professions with regard to the role of the professional association. In many countries associations of officers and non-coms are formed, but these devote themselves primarily to the material interests of their members. They play no role in the development of the military profession; they presuppose its existence and, in doing so, confirm it.

Compared with most professions, the professionalization of the military shows a different sequence of events: commission, monopoly, a high social status and a code of ethics have come first; the establishment of training schools followed, rather slowly in the oldest branches of service; professional associations played only a minor role.

Our problem now is, to what extent do the military profession and the military organization agree with each other; in other words, how far has the integration of both patterns progressed, given the development of each as sketched above in a specific course in time.

THE FUSION OF PROFESSION AND ORGANIZATION

The present interpenetration of professional and organizational controls does not always lead to the same result. If professionalization became established earlier than organization of conduct, it has a better chance to survive the fusion of the two. The same holds true in the case where the organization of conduct is established first. Once it is institutionalized, the subsequent infusion with the new control structure can be better endured.[30]

In the case of the officer, there can be no doubt of the historical sequence. Military organization has established its form centuries before professionalization definitely began. The hierarchy of rank, backbone of military organization, included officers from the begining.[31] This excludes the possibility of fraternal equality as it is usually found among professionals. Career orientation, the central characteristic of bureaucrats, is traditionally part and parcel of the military institution.

The historical priority of organization over profession, and the domination of organizational controls, may easily be explained by the function of the armed forces. Warfare not only demands large-scale organization, but, moreover, an extreme instrumentalization of social relations. The name of Passchendaele stands as a modern symbol of this rigorous instrumentalism.[32]

Both the sequence of organizational and professional tendencies and the functional requirements of modern warfare seem to offer small possibilities for professionalism. Yet in the course of the nineteenth century the military profession is clearly established. Without any doubt, the officer corps shows a number of important professional characteristics.

This leads to the key problem: how to explain the fact that professionalization has broken through the barriers of organization and instrumentalization?

We believe that the successful professionalization of the armed forces must, first of all, be explained by the intervention of the state. Military professionalization was a process of *forced and planned professionalization*.

Among the professions, the armed services occupy a unique position in that the state is their client. This implies the reversibility of the relation between service and client: being the superior power in the nation-state, the client-government as a monopolist has so great an interest in the smooth functioning of the service-institute that it subjects it to a set of rules.

This explains the remarkable sequence in the gradual process of military professionalization: it has not been struggled for by the military, it has not even been willed by them. It was imposed by the "client" who, in his own interest, assigned commissions and established training schools.

The fact is easily proved that the officership, especially that of the traditional non-technical arms, even opposed progressive professionalization.[33] The aristocratic heritage proved one of the main barriers to attempts to elevate the level of the officer corps by a more rigorous selection and a scientific training. These attempts were rightly interpreted as an endeavour to change military leadership from an ascribed role into an achieved one.

Yet, on the other hand, the common aristocratic origin and the accompanying sense of belonging to an elite were the very weapons to be used against the menace of organizational instrumentalism. They affirmed the exclusiveness and the solidarity of the officer corps, and so held the upper hand over the simultaneous process of rank-hierarchization.

The high social status of the officer, moreover, had its parallel in the social structure of the armed forces. Prior to and within the nineteenth century, army personnel consisted chiefly of proletarian elements, often crimped or even—in the navy—pressed into service, or reared in traditional submission to the bearers of authority.

This differential social origin of officers and men in earlier centuries has led to a sharp dichotomy in the military forces. Continual organization and hierarchization have robbed the officers of part of their autonomy; however, they have been able to maintain a sharp distinction between themselves and the lower ranks. This distinction has acquired a latent function by serving as a basis of the officers' conviction to belong to a responsible and privileged group. The combination of profession and organization in the army has thus been institutionalized in two ways: in a fusion on the level of the officer corps, and in a simultaneous segregation of both patterns in the army as a whole by a sharp division between officers and men.

This dichotomy might endanger the functioning of the military forces, if the army was not part of an institution *strongly isolated from society.*

This isolation, which exceeds the normal institutionalized division of labor in modern societies may be explained especially by the very exceptional function of the army: the conduct of war, respectively, the preparation for war. This function is so exceptional and therefore differs so sharply from other institutions which ensure the continuity of society, that the standing armies were distinctly isolated from the rest of society, locally, socially, and culturally; in ethos, ideology, ritual and dress.

This situation strongly fostered the integration of all sections of the armed forces as well as the emergence of a specific military culture. In this way the fusion of organization and profession was affirmed, with both centred on the military craft. The barrier between the military and the civilian is higher than the barrier between officers and men.

The distinction between officers and men is certainly not simply the outcome of a historical process. Rather, it is a functional distinction: the military profession is traditionally and actually a *managerial profession.* The presence of numerous specialists in the army, both within and outside the officer corps, does not alter the fact that the central skill and the distinct sphere of officership is, in Lasswell's phrase "the management of violence." "The direction, operation, and control of a human organization whose primary function is the application of violence is the peculiar skill of the officer. It is common to the activities of the air, land, and sea officers."[34]

This relatively exceptional characteristic of the professional soldier implies that the tension between managerial and expertise roles which is also found in other professions is accepted here *a priori*. Managerial and professional skill, bureaucratic and professional authority coincide in many respects.

The officer, moreover, as an officer, always remains in a closed community. Officership is not a free profession; neither is it incorporated in diverging services and organizations; but it is, again in a unique way, a *concentrated profession*.

With respect to the relation between profession and organization this means that the profession, by definition, is itself an organization. The officer corps is not a corps in the sense in which a medical corps, a university staff, or a professional association are one. It implies both professional and organizational roles and patterns, which embrace all members of the profession.

Hence the late emergence and the relatively small significance of associations of officers. Traditionally, the officer found his professional community *in* his corporate organization.

Together with historical origin and institutional isolation, this concentration in one corps gives the armed forces, until now, the characteristics of a "relatively closed community where professional and residential life have been completely intermingled."[35] Hence, some professional institutions in the past resembled Goffman's "total institutions."[36]

The old-style military academy is a good example. Professional training not only took place within a very strictly disciplined and isolated community, but the school itself has been fully integrated in the military organization as a whole.

Unlike most other professions, professional training here already completely conforms to patterns which anticipate managerial roles in the organization. The academy, moreover, has its year groups, important socializing group agencies, which arrange cadets during their professional training in hierarchical units.

Because professional training is a key mechanism in the process of professional socialization and, therefore, in the profession as such, this emphatic integration in the military establishment and its hierarchy is of the greatest importance for the fusion of profession and organization.[37] The organization of professional socialization makes the officer corps an *organized profession*.

The above mentioned more or less unique characteristics of the military profession together offer a sufficient explanation of the successful fusion of professional and organizational controls in a single pattern. At the same time, they point to the weakness of this fusion, because during the last decades those very conditions of existence were being undermined.

First, state control has become an anti-professional influence as a result of the penetration of ideology in national and international politics. The politicalization of the armed forces, which began in the totalitarian states during the interwar period, after the Second World War spread to many countries which had taken sides in the Cold War between East and West.[38] This process involves a fusion of military and political commitments which threatens the traditional ideological neutrality so characteristic of the professions.

Second, the elite status of the officer has almost completely disappeared as a result of a marked shift to middle class recruitment. The social and cultural basis of the distinction between officers and men has been undermined, if it has not disappeared altogether. This tendency is being strengthened by the democratization of Western society and the decline of the isolation of the military institution and its key organizations.

Third, the homogeneous managerial role of the officer is subjected to frequent role differentiation as a consequence of specialization. At the higher levels, increasing interservice competition and controversy may be observed.[39] At the lower levels there is an ever growing specialization of skill and knowledge. All the same, the officer faces increasing competition of civilian experts, which according to Colonel Ginsburgh is "the most important aspect of the challenge to military professionalism."[40]

One may even ask whether military leadership and management will remain, in the long run, the hard core of the officer's function. Even where this still is the case, often as a consequence of modern guerilla warfare,[41] he is nevertheless at the lower and middle levels, much more the leader of a combat unit than the representative of an authoritarian caste of commanders.

In sociological terms, this process is a decisive phase in the development from mechanical into organic solidarity, to use Durkheim's well-known dichotomy.[42] The officer caste and the closed formations or two-deep line of *tirailleurs,* standing shoulder to shoulder, are replaced by specialized, integrated, relatively autonomous combat units. Functional authority replaces status domination.[43]

CONCLUSIONS

We must now ask whether the interpretation of professional and organization control patterns is threatened by these developments. Is the military profession with its traditional relation to bureaucratic roles in "danger" of disruption?

We believe that there is no question of deprofessionalization. On the contrary, the final disappearance of elite-ascription and the intensification of scientific training more likely indicate the completion of an unfinished process of professionalization. The same holds for the debates on the relation between the armed forces, politics and larger society, which can only serve to clarify and to further the awareness of the social role of the military.

In the same way, the compelling international military cooperation (NATO) may be regarded as the beginning of the liberation of the officer corps from the narrowness of nationalism, and in any case as a possibility to reorientate the military profession as such.

The attempts to politicize the army, as well as the penetration by civilians into areas which were traditionally reserved to the military, may in fact be seen as counteracting traditional professionalism, but they will not necessarily prove fatal to professional autonomy. In any case, the growing social and ideological awareness and the necessity to enter into discussions with civilian experts eliminates the dangers of a bureaucratic caste feeling in profession and organization.

These changes in the military profession will doubtless influence the organizational control pattern. They have sometimes been expressly brought about to answer the demands of the military organization for socio-technical skill and flexibility.

It cannot be denied that all this leads to uncertainty and even disorientation in conduct and attitude. When an old profession, anchored in a traditional organization, is subjected to radical changes, such feelings cannot be avoided.

We have, however, the certainty that new patterns of profession and organization will develop, especially in the traditionally bureaucratic professions. What the professional soldier has always tried to combine, at present emerges in other occupational institutions as the beginning of a new combination. The professional and organizational revolution of our time destroys neither the one nor the other, but only the old formulas: "the occupational group of the future will combine elements from both the professional and bureaucratic models; the average professional man will combine professional and non-professional orientations; [. . .] mixed forms of control, hybrid organizations are the likely outcomes."[44]

The armed forces have some historical and actual experience in the processes of fusing and mixing professional and organizational solutions. Their experiences can serve as a model or a warning for those who are today confronted with the necessity to find new formulas.

NOTES

[1]Peter M. Blau and W. Richard Scott, *Formal Organizations—A Comparative Approach* (San Francisco: Chandler, 1962), 60 ff.

[2]Heinz Hartmann, *Funktionale Autorität: Systematische Abhandlung zu einem soziologischen Begriff* (Stuttgart: Enke, 1964), 18 ff.

[3]Robert K. Merton, "Patterns of Influence: Local and Cosmopolitan Influentials," *Social Theory and Social Structure* (Glencoe: The Free Press, 1957, 2nd ed.), 387-420; Alvin W. Gouldner, "Cosmopolitans and Locals: Toward an Analysis of Latent Social Roles," *Administrative Science Quarterly*, Vol. II (1957-58), 281-306 and 444-80.

[4]Harold L. Wilensky, "The Professionalization of Everyone?," *The American Journal of Sociology*, Vol. LXX (1964), 146.

[5]Blau and Scott, *op. cit.*, 64-74; Wilensky, *op. cit.*, 146-58; Amitai Etzioni, *A Comparative Analysis of Complex Organizations* (N.Y.: The Free Press of Glencoe, 1961), 257-61.

[6]Samuel P. Huntington, *The Soldier and the State: The Theory and Politics of Civil-Military Relations* (Cambridge: Harvard University Press, 1959), 469: "This author has discovered only one volume in English which analyzes officership as a profession: Michael Lewis, England's Sea Officers: The Story of the Naval Profession (London 1939) (. . .) Sociological studies, following Max Weber, have usually analyzed the military as a bureaucratic structure." Wilensky, *op. cit.*, 141, 143.

[7]Huntington, *op. cit.*, 11-18; Morris Janowitz, *The Professional Soldier* (Glencoe: The Free Press, 1960), 215-25.

[8]Huntington, *ibid.*, 16.

[9]Huntington, *ibid.*, 17, 74 ff.

[10]J. A. A. v. Doorn, *Sociologie van de organisatie* (Leiden: Stenfert Kroese, 1956), 34-45.

[11]Michael Roberts, *The Military Revolution 1560-1660* (Inaugural Lecture, Queen's University of Belfast, 1956. Private circulation), 11.

[12]Eugen von Frauenholz, *Das Heerwesen des Reiches in der Landsknechtszeit* (München, 1937), 26, 41 ff; Idem, *Das Söldnertum in der Zeit des Dreissigjährigen Krieges* (München, 1958), 11.

[13]Werner Hahlweg, *Die Heeresreform der Oranier und die Antike* (Berlin, 1941), 32 ff.

[14]Roberts, *op. cit.*, 9.

[15]Hahlweg, *op. cit.*, 191: 'Niemals vorher noch nachher ist eine derart fruchtbare und volkommene Aufnahme von Lehren des griechisch-römischen Altertums in irgendeine Zeitabschnitt nachweisbar.'

[16]Huntington, *op. cit.*, 20; Fritz Redlich, 'The Military Enterpriser: A Neglected Area of Research', *Explorations in Entrepreneurial History*, VIII (1956), 252-56.

[17]Von Frauenholz, 'Heerwesen', *op. cit.*, 26: 'Wenn sich die Artikel des Fussvolks gegen Ungehorsam und Meuterei wenden, so wird im Reiterrecht gegen das Unternehmertum Front gemacht.'

[18]Max Weber, *Wirtschaft und Gesellschaft* (Tübingen: Mohr, 1925, 2nd ed.), 665.

45

[19]Redlich, *op. cit.*, 255 ff.

[20]Michael Lewis, *A Social History of the Navy 1793-1815* (London: Allen & Unwin, 1960), 40.

[21]Lewis, *op. cit.*, 150.

[22]Wilensky, *op. cit.*, 142 ff.

[23]Von Frauenholz, 'Söldnertum,' *op. cit.*, 34 f.

[24]Roberts, *op. cit.*, 24; Victor Loewe, *Die Organisation und Verwaltung der Wallensteinschen Heere* (Freiburg i.B. und Leipzig: Mohr, 1895), 85 f.

[25]Portepee: ornamental tassel of the sabre.

[26]Huntington, *op. cit.*, 24 f.; B. Poten, *Geschichte des Militär-Erziehungs und Bildungswesens in den Landen Deutscher Zunge,* Vol. I (Berlin, 1889), 4 ff., 53 ff.; Lewis, *op. cit.*, 143 ff.

[27]Karl Demeter, *Das Deutsche Offizierkorps in Gesellschaft und Staat, 1650-1945* (Frankfurt am Main: Bernard und Graefe, 1962), 10.

[28]Janowitz, *op. cit.*, 94; Demeter, *op. cit.*, ch. I; François Bédarida, L'armée et la République: les opinions politiques des officiers français en 1876-78, *Revue historique,* Vol. LXXXVIII/232 (1964), 151 ff.

[29]Janowitz, *op. cit.*, 95 f; Demeter, *op. cit.*, 52 ff.

[30]Wilensky, *op. cit.*, 156: 'To the degree that professionalization is the expedient adoption of professional forms in a struggle for prestige and income, the fact that someone—layman, manager, or professional—got there first is central.'

[31]Roberts, *op. cit.*, 28: 'The first half of the seventeenth century sees the real emergence of the concept of rank'; Loewe, *op. cit.*, 19.

[32]M. D. Feld, 'Information and Authority: The Structure of Military Organization,' *American Sociological Review,* Vol. XXIV (1959), 15-22.

[33]Demeter, *op. cit.*, 69 ff; Lewis, *op. cit.*, 142 ff.

[34]Huntington, *op. cit.*, 11.

[35]Janowitz, *op. cit.*, 177 f.

[36]Erving Goffman, 'On the Characteristics of Total Institutions: The Inmate World', in Donald R. Cressey (ed.), *The Prison: Studies in Institutional Organization and Change* (New York: Holt, Rinehart and Winston, 1961), 16 ff.

[37]C. J. Lammers, *Het Koninklijk Instituut voor de Marine. Een Sociologische Analyse van de Inlijving van Groepen Aspirant-Officieren in de Zeemacht* (Assen: Van Gorcum, 1963), ch. VII and XIII.

[38]Janowitz, *op. cit.*, ch. XIII, XIV, XV; Huntington, *op. cit.*, 116: 'An "unpolitical army" is an intolerable anomaly in a completely politicized totalitarian society'; S. E. Finer, *The Man on Horseback: The Role of the Military in Politics* (London and Dunmow: Pall Mall Press, 1962).

[39]Samuel P. Huntington, 'Interservice Competition and the Political Roles of the Armed Services', *The American Political Science Review,* Vol. LV (1961), 40-52.

[40]Robert N. Ginsburg, 'The Challenge to Military Professionalism,' *Foreign Affairs,* Vol. XLII (1964), 258-60.

[41]Raoul Girardet (ed.), *La crise militaire francaise, 1945-1962: Aspects sociologiques et idéologiques* (Paris: Armand Colin, 1964), 22, 223.

[42]Emile Durkheim, *The Division of Labor in Society* (Glencoe: The Free Press, 1947).

[43]Janowitz, *op. cit.*, 8 ff., 38 ff.

[44]Wilensky, *op. cit.*, 157.

Part Two

THE MILITARY

IN MODERN SOCIETY

Chapter 3

THE DECLINE OF THE MASS ARMY

INTRODUCTION

*A*t first sight it might seem ironic to speak of the decline of the mass army in this day and age, when peace-time armed forces are greater and defence expenditure is higher than ever before. In 1970[1] an estimated 23,000,000 men were on active military service throughout the world and total military expenditure amounted to more than US $200,000,000,000. The armed forces of individual states may also be described as mass forces. As far as the super powers are concerned it is well known that in 1973 the armed forces of the United States consisted of 2.2 million men, those of the Soviet Union 3.4 million, and those of Communist China 2.9 million. But other countries have large standing armies as well. West Germany, Italy and Turkey each have more than 400,000 men, and France has more than 500,000. Nor do the very poor countries lag far behind, as is apparent from India's almost one million men, and Indonesia's 322,000.

It is nevertheless the case that a number of West European countries have gradually reduced their military manpower, as may be seen from Table 1.

This trend is not the principal reason, however, for speaking in terms of the decline of the mass army. For it is not solely, or even primarily, a question of a reduction in total manpower. Of greater interest is the fact that the basis of the mass army, viz., the system of general conscription, is being subjected to increasing pressure and plans for an all-volunteer force are becoming more definite in a

51

Table 1. Comparison of military manpower[2]

	1964	1968	1973
Belgium	110,000	99,000	89,600
Britain	425,000	427,000	361,500
Denmark	52,000	46,000	39,800
France	620,000	505,000	503,000
Netherlands	124,000	129,000	112,200
Norway	37,000	35,000	35,900

number of countries. The United States, for instance, decided five years ago, in 1970, to switch to a voluntary armed force, a decision in which it was preceded in West Europe by the United Kingdom. France and the Netherlands have similar plans and many countries have now begun to limit conscription both as regards manpower and the conscription period.

Underlying these trends is the more fundamental problem of the declining legitimacy of the armed forces, which is more apparent in some countries than in others. It is reflected with particular clarity in the reaction of the younger generation to conscription, and there is a feeling in many Western countries that the armed forces are facing a crisis as a result of their increasing unpopularity with the public.

Partly for this reason the West is availing itself of the opportunity to utilize the diminution of international tension between NATO and the Warsaw Pact for the mutual and balanced force reductions on which talks have been in progress for some years now. Even if military expenditures continue to rise or remain at the same level the number of men and weapons will almost certainly go down, for manpower costs have become too high.[3] Attempts will be made to cut these costs, which can only be done through reductions in manpower size.

It may be wondered, even by those who are familiar with these facts, whether we are not in fact dealing with yet another of many fluctuations in the size of the armed forces, this time brought about by a temporary détente. Though détente is certainly a factor, it is by no means the only one. It looks as though the Western world has now reached a historic stage in which the mass army as an institution is on the way out. It is not a political-cyclical trend, but a structural change spelling the end of a process which began with the French Revolution and the national revolutions of the early nineteenth century. The mass army came into being with the rise of nationalism, when the right to bear arms was regarded as one of the principal acquisitions of the new national citizenry. General conscription was a means of ensuring the continued existence of the mass army.

This period of history is now coming to an end. "The nation in arms" is an obsolete conception. The armed forces have steadily evolved into an instrument of deterrence with a high degree of technical specialization which holds little attraction for the young people of today. Nuclear weapons and international blocs have replaced the nation in arms. The former expansionism of the Western states has disappeared, at least in its military form.

We could go still further and conclude with Teitler that the historical alternation of absolute and instrumental armed conflict has now taken a turn in the direction of the latter. This implies the limiting or, if possible, the avoidance of conflict; it is in any case institutionalization. The armed forces are consequently inclined to monopolize and professionalize the use of force, which they are also capable of doing. This turn gives rise to a preference for volunteer forces and for a general reduction in the armed forces.[4]

After an analysis of the concept "mass army" two related problems will be discussed: the reduction of the draft and the social isolation of an all-volunteer armed force.

THE MASS ARMY: SIZE, HOMOGENEITY, MOBILIZATION

Analysis of the term "mass army" may help to clarify the problem. For the word "mass" has at least three different meanings, one indicating size, one indicating homogeneity and one indicating a social entity characterized by social mobilization. The first meaning might seem to be the most obvious one in this context, but it is less important than the others. "Mass army" was first used in connection with the large-scale armed forces which governed military operations in the nineteenth century. Though sixteenth- and seventeenth-

century armies never consisted of more than a hundred thousand
men, Napoleon raised an army of a million men at the peak of his
military effort. In the years between the First and Second World
Wars the big powers maintained armies of more than half a million
or even a million men.

This increase in size is closely connected with the nationalization and democratization of the military. The *levée en masse* of the
French Revolution was continued in the system of general conscription which gave rise to the concept of *Volk in Waffen,* or a nation in
arms. So the mass army is quite rightly seen in relation to the draft.[5]
Only very big and very wealthy countries can afford large volunteer
armies in peace time, and even the United States was compelled to
incorporate a drastic and continuing reduction in manpower level
in its recent change-over to a standing all-volunteer force. In 1970
estimates were at the level of a volunteer force of 2.4 million. That
figure had dropped to 2.23 million by 1973, while current thinking
is along the lines of 2 million in 1975 and even 1.75 million in the
longer term.[6]

Since in conscript forces the percentage of volunteers is significantly lower in the army (land forces) than in the navy or air force,
it is understandable that the study of a reduction in military forces
should be restricted to the decline of the mass *army.* Reduction of
the armed forces is always to the detriment of the army. It is equally
true that "the more a country relies on conscripted manpower the
more clearly is its armed force dominated by the Army."[7]

If ending conscription means a smaller army then the reverse
is also true because reduction of the army necessitates the introduction of a selected service system which would amount to inequitable
burden-sharing and would therefore hasten the end of conscription.

"Mass army" can also be understood to mean an army with a
highly undifferentiated and homogeneous composition. Historical
formations of foot soldiers, such as the Roman legions, the Spanish
tertios and the Prussian battalions, are extreme examples of this
kind of homogeneity. Comparatively speaking, the infantry is still
less differentiated and internally specialized than the rest of the
army. Its characteristic is uniformity in skills and behavior. The
decline of the mass army can therefore be regarded as a diminution
of this unspecialised mass characteristic. Studies like those by Wool

and Lang[8] have shown there to be a strong tendency towards continuing specialization in the land forces as well. The rifleman has long ceased to be the prototype of the soldier.

This goes together with a heavy increase in the number of non-combatant functions in the occupational structure of the army, accompanied by a higher administrative density. The gradual specialization and bureaucratization of the military is another indication of the decline of the mass army. Much of this trend is attributable to the technological advances in military operations. Increased firepower and improved means of communication and transportation demand more highly qualified and specialized manpower. Though warfare still involves hundreds of thousands of people, modern battlefields no longer feature huge masses of men but are empty, just as the plant floor is empty in so many modern industrial concerns. Mechanization and specialization are having their effect on industry as well, and like the mass of infantry in the army the mass of workers in the industrial plant is making way for small groups of highly qualified technicians. In this sense the decline of the mass army may be said to run parallel to the decline of the mass plant.

A third meaning of "mass" is that found in terms like mass culture, mass media and mass democracy.[9] Feld has pointed out that in this sense mass armies have contributed to the emergence of mass societies, i.e., societies capable of mobilizing their members for large-scale collective objectives. This describes the relation between the mass army and mass movements—clearly perceptible in Communist China and Castroist Cuba—on the one hand, and between the mass army and the totalitarian state on the other. Kirchheimer is of the opinion that the First World War, a war of mass armies par excellence, taught the political leaders how to mobilize great masses of people and resources, a technique which was later utilized in peace time for domestic purposes.[10]

Viewed in this context, the decline of the mass army may be regarded as a diminution of the power of political elites to command the uncritical support of the population when anything in the nature of a collective effort is to be made. This implies a lessening of the possibility of commanding popular support for a political course of collective militancy and naive patriotism. The armed forces seem to be reassuming the role of a functional instrument of force, after a century of being a major channel for mass hysteria and mass politics.

The present day individualism, subjectivism and hedonism are contributing factors. To the youth of the industrialised countries the military is not doing his duty but merely doing his job. The declining legitimacy of the national state helps to discredit the army as a national institution par excellence, just as the draft is an enemy of the institution of the national state. Regarded more and more as coercion, the draft is a symbol of the reduced legitimacy of the state.[11]

THE END OF THE DRAFT?

As we have seen, the history of the mass army is directly connected with the institution of the draft. Though wars sometimes produce large temporary armies of volunteers, and revolutions sometimes call forth mass armies of militia forces, it is nevertheless the case that standing armies of considerable size are only possible with a system of conscription: the size of the army is an inverse function of the volunteer / conscript ratio.[12]

It remains a moot point, however, whether plans for military force reduction can go so far as to make the draft completely redundant. The available data show that all-volunteer forces experience considerable difficulty in recruiting the best possible men in sufficient numbers. On the whole, it is difficult to find qualified personnel for professional military activities in the developed countries. This being the case, the decline of the mass army is not expected to lead inevitably to the end of the draft unless international relations can be eased to the point where much smaller armies than those currently planned will be sufficient.

The growing public criticism of the draft, however, and more especially the resistance of the younger generation, have placed the policy-makers under continuous pressure, which explains their plans to redefine the draft in terms of national service, i.e., to transform the military into a force with emergency and domestic tasks.[13]

This policy will be difficult to carry out in a number of West

European countries, where anti-militarism is now so strong that the assumption of non-military tasks by the military would be interpreted as a transparent attempt to preserve an obsolete—and expensive—institution. What might be termed goal succession would be interpreted as goal displacement, or reversing the ends and means in an attempt to safeguard the existing organization. It is impossible to define new organizational goals when the old ones are no longer acceptable. Moreover, in those countries the social-economic field is fully occupied by civil organizations, which are constantly on their guard against encroachments by rival organizations. Only a society with institutional lacunae provides opportunities for using an organization like the military for domestic purposes.

It may thus be concluded that the present tendency to reduce the draft will continue, though it will not culminate in the end of the draft in all cases. It is a process with important consequences for recruitment and the social composition of the armed forces. Changing over to a volunteer army means first and foremost a transition from compulsory enrolment to orientation towards the labor market. It being unlikely that moral involvement and professional preference will be found in sufficient quantity, economic incentives will become increasingly necessary to fill the ranks. Payment, work conditions, career prospects and pensions will become the main points of attraction. In times of full employment this will give rise to keen competition with civilian occupations, assuming of course that the generous material rewards offered attract the requisite numbers. The convergence between a number of military and civilian jobs will make it more difficult to activate motives other than those prevailing in the civilian world of work.

For the performance of military duties, which is more than simply working for money, this means a move in the direction of a force of mercenaries, and this in turn will adversely affect not only the way the military themselves experience their profession but also the public image of the armed forces.[14]

A second consequence of orientation towards the labor market is a decline in the social representativeness of the armed forces. Conscription means that a cross section of the whole population goes into the armed forces, with the exception of those who are physically or mentally unsuitable. An all-volunteer force will be dependent on the [heavily segmented] labor market, which will mean that some segments will be more readily accessible than others. Serious problems will occur if moreover ethnic minorities are over-represented on the accessible markets. This point is currently the subject of discussion in the United States, where it is feared that a disproportionate number of blacks will join the all-volunteer force. Broadly speaking, deprived social categories may be expected to supply proportionately more personnel, with the concomitant risk of a poor man's army, which would not be consistent with the national task of the armed forces or with the risks attached to war.

West-European countries without ethnic minorities of any significance will on the other hand experience great difficulty in filling the lower ranks with volunteers. For the type of job concerned is that held in industry by hundreds of thousands of foreign workers (migrant labor), an example which the armed forces can hardly be expected to follow.

A further probable consequence of the change-over to a volunteer force is an over-representation of personnel with a conservative outlook. This would mean a complete break with the present political and social orientation of draftees who, in view of their age, education and youth culture, may be termed left-wing. In one respect, namely in educational level, the present incongruency in the social composition of the army would be improved. The secondary education of the majority of the present-day younger generation means that most conscripts are better educated than non-commissioned officers, while some even have higher educational qualifications than some of the regular officers.[15] A volunteer army would replace the two pyramids of regulars and conscripts with one pyramid of volunteers trained to the level required. In other words, the organizational functional hierarchy would more or less coincide with the stratification along educational lines.

A third consequence of orientation towards the labor market is the inevitable penetration of the values and norms prevailing in civilian industrial and labor relations, including tendencies towards unionization. The fear that an all-volunteer force will assume caste-like characteristics can probably be discounted for countries with a weak military tradition. The chance may be greater that industrial patterns will be copied on a large scale. The fact that military unionism is now on the increase, even among conscripts, is an indication of this.

A STATE WITHIN THE STATE?

The foregoing serves as an introduction to a brief examination of the different set of relations between the armed forces and the social environment, namely the civil-military relations. The principal question here is whether the decline of the mass army will affect the incorporation of the armed forces in society.

It is generally assumed that the main effect will be a wider gap between the military and the civilian sectors. A smaller military force—and certainly an all-volunteer one—will have less contact with the community. It will be more inner-directed and perhaps more rigid because of the slowing down or even the discontinuance of the flow of large numbers of conscripts. At the same time, as we have already noted, the political composition will become more one-sided, with an inclination towards conservative thinking.[16]

It is above all this expectation of greater rigidity and conservatism which is helping to postpone reduction of the draft in many West European countries. It is especially prevalent among those political circles and parties for whom military prestige is low and who are highly critical of the military. It is as though draftees in the armed forces are regarded as a countervailing power against a right-wing professional elite. An all-volunteer force is referred to as a state within the state, and occasionally the fear is expressed that an army of this kind could proceed to political intervention.

It should be stated here that no simple link between military professionalism and military intervention in politics has to date been shown to exist. Huntington is even of the opinion that a high degree of military professionalism will lead to the adoption of a politically neutral position and to acceptance of full control by the civilian government.[17] Though experience in many modern states supports this view, it is contradicted by many new nations where highly professionalized armies seize political power and establish a military regime. Obviously, the chance of military intervention is influenced not only by the degree of professionalization, but also by what Finer terms the level of political culture.[18]

Another point of interest here is the doubt expressed by Janowitz regarding the view that the democratization of the officer corps in terms of the social origin of its members provides some guarantee that it will not proceed to undemocratic action.[19] Recent empirical research by Kourvetaris and Dobratz supports his doubts on this score.[20]

Broadly speaking, it may be observed that in mass armies the military elite has always consisted of regular officers with a preponderantly conservative outlook and that it is always this elite, and not the rank and file, which takes decisions regarding political action and social pressure. This is not to say of course that the chance of institutional rigidity will not increase in an all-volunteer force. If an army of this kind does not become a state within the state it can still become a closed organization within the surrounding society.

For this reason it is important that planning for the decline of the mass army be accompanied by planning for countervailing civilian power. This would include appointing qualified civilians to political top positions in the Ministry of Defence, more parliamentary experts in military affairs, training military specialists in the universities and technical colleges, and shorter careers for part of the professional personnel.

This is not a plea for civilianization. The decline of the mass army can be regarded without difficulty as re-militarization in the sense that the many social functions of the traditional mass army— school of the nation, embodiment of masculine virtues—will disappear because the purely instrumental and functional characteristics of the military will then come more fully into their own. An all-volunteer force can be more technocratic than the mass army has ever been. Modern weapon systems also play a part here in that technical weapons—and quite certainly nuclear weapons—no longer provide points of contact for mass involvement and ideological inspiration. Missile systems are not easy to combine with aggressive militarism. They guarantee international security, but cannot be pressed into the service of neo-nationalist ideologies.[21]

In this sense the separation of men and weapons is a positive development. What has been deplored from the days of Marx onwards as alienation in industry—the separation of the worker from the means of production—has achieved positive results in the military sphere, where alienation is a protective wall against a popular and populistic militarism.

If the present détente in Europe continues, interest will remain focussed on the question of defence with fewer men. If it moves no further ahead the fact will still remain that the era of mass armies is past. The defence of the West will depend more and more on military techniques functioning within the framework of new types of policy, strategy and organization. What is true of so many crucial social questions is also true of the armed forces: the mass deployment of manpower is no longer the solution.

NOTES

[1] *World Military Expenditures 1970*. Publication 58 of the United States Arms Control and Disarmament Agency (Washington D.C.: US Government Printing Office, 1970), 1 and 6.

[2] *World Military Expenditures 1970, op. cit.,* 26 ff. *The Military Balance 1973-1974* (London: The International Institute for Strategic Studies, 1973), 77.

[3] Kenneth Hunt, *The Alliance and Europe: Part II, Defence with Fewer Men.* Adelphi Paper No. 98 (London: The International Institute for Strategic Studies, 1973), 9.

[4] Ger Teitler, *Toepassing van geweld* (The Application of Force) (Meppel: Boom, 1972), 18-34.

[5] M. R. D. Foot, *Men in Uniform: Military Manpower in Modern Industrial Societies* (London: The International Institute for Strategic Studies, 1961), 32 ff.; Erwin Häckel, *Military Manpower and Political Purpose.* Adelphi Paper No. 72 (London: The International Institute for Strategic Studies, 1970), 5: 'The relative size of the Army . . . tends to be inversely proportional to the percentage of volunteers among the total armed personnel.' Also: 'In conscript forces the percentage of volunteers is significantly lower in the Army (land force) than in the armed services as a whole. Conversely, there is always a higher proportion of volunteers among the other services.'

[6] Morris Janowitz, *The U.S. Forces and the Zero Draft.* Adelphi Paper No. 94 (London: The International Institute for Strategic Studies, 1973), 7.

[7] Häckel, *op. cit.,* 5.

[8] Harold Wool, *The Military Specialist. Skilled Manpower for the Armed Forces* (Baltimore: The John Hopkins Press, 1968); Kurt Lang, 'Trends in the Military Occupational Structure and Their Political Implications', *Journal of Political and Military Sociology,* Vol. I, No. 1 (1973), 1-18.

[9] William Kornhauser, *The Politics of Mass Society* (New York: The Free Press, 1959); Daniel Bell, *The End of Ideology* (New York: The Free Press, 1961), See ch. I: 'America as a Mass Society: A Critique'.

[10] O. Kirchheimer, 'Confining Conditions and Revolutionary Breakthroughs', *The American Political Science Review,* Vol. LIX (1965), 973.

[11] Kenneth E. Boulding, 'The Impact of the Draft on the Legitimacy of the National State', in Sol Tax (ed.), *The Draft: A Handbook of Facts and Alternatives* (Chicago and London: The University of Chicago Press, 1967), 195 ff.

[12] Häckel, *op. cit.,* 12.

[13] An interesting collection of essays in *Teachers College Record,* Vol. LXXIII, No. 1 (September 1971), with contributions from Morris Janowitz, Charles C. Moskos, Jr., Albert D. Biderman *et al.*

[14] Gwyn Harries-Jenkins, 'From Conscription to Volunteer Armies', *Force in Modern Societies: The Military Profession.* Adelphi Paper No. 103 (London: The International Institute for Strategic Studies, 1973), 13.

[15] A few Dutch figures (1970): 12% of the draftees had only primary education while 72% of military jobs for draftees required nothing higher than this level. 16% of the draftees were college or university graduates, while only 2% of military jobs were at that level.

[16] Morris Janowitz, *op. cit.,* 27.

[17]Samuel P. Huntington, *The Soldier and the State: The Theory and Politics of Civil-Military Relations* (Cambridge, Mass.: Harvard University Press, 1957), 83 ff.

[18]S. E. Finer, *The Man on Horseback: The Role of the Military in Politics* (London and Dunmow: Pall Mall Press, 1962), 87 ff.; Jacques van Doorn, 'Political Change and the Control of the Military', in Jacques van Doorn (ed.), *Military Profession and Military Regimes: Commitments and Conflicts* (The Hague and Paris: Mouton, 1969), 26-31.

[19]Morris Janowitz, *The Professional Soldier: A Social and Political Portrait* (New York: The Free Press, 1960), 10 ff.

[20]George A. Kourvetaris and Betty A. Dobratz, 'Social Recruitment and Political Orientations of the Officer Corps in a Comparative Perspective', *Pacific Sociological Review,* Vol. XVI, No. 2 (April 1973), 228-54.

[21]Gerd Schmückle, *Kommiss a.D.: Kritische Gänge durch die Kasernen* (Stuttgart: Seewald Verlag, 1971), 45.

Chapter 4

POLITICAL CHANGE AND THE CONTROL OF THE MILITARY

INTRODUCTION

*T*he political control of the armed forces has been the subject of investigation on many occasions and in many contexts. This is quite understandable in view of the peculiar character of the military institution, being the most powerful force in the state and yet, at the same time, its main instrument in latent and manifest conflicts with other states.

In this article, however, a special aspect of the general problem will be discussed: the control of the military under conditions of fundamental and rapid political change. It is under such conditions that the opportunity for the military to move into the political field is obviously very great. At that moment the capacity of the political regime to withstand the pressure of the military is tested much stronger than under normal conditions.

Two processes of fundamental political change will be compared. On the one hand the take-over of a regime by a new one, as has been demonstrated in a number of Eastern European countries. On the other hand the emergence of new nations, where colonial rule has given way to an independent political regime.

At first sight the two types of nation would seem to display too wide a diversity of traits to permit a comparative analysis. It cannot be stressed enough that many of the new socialist countries belong to the developed political systems, whereas the other new nations are countries of low or minimal political culture.[1] In addition, the ideological nature of the two types of state differs considerably.

The experience common to both types of systems is, nevertheless, their complete break with the old political order and their consequent need to create entirely new civil-military relations. The
problem they share may be defined as *the ability of the political elite
to control the armed forces despite radical changes in the political
order*. This being so, it is not so much the transfer of authority to the
armed forces which is of interest, but rather the political control of
the military in a given process of power transfer.

Though this problem is of practical importance, it has an even
greater theoretical significance, since the concept of military professionalism, like every other kind of professionalism, includes a peren-
nial search for autonomy which is in contradiction to tight political
control. Rapid social and political change, however, would seem to
make it imperative, sometimes even a condition for survival, for the
political sphere to maintain a strong grip on the armed forces. A
succession of divergent political systems can perhaps make manifest
the potential incompatibility of political and professional values,
criteria and roles. The succession-crisis may be expected to pare
down the authority structure to the underlying frame of naked
power.

Tensions in civil-military relations are not a recent phenomenon.
Modern revolutions, coups, and the sudden emergence of independent nations, however, obviously have a much greater impact on
the established relations between politics and the armed forces than
the gradual introduction of the system of royal commissions and of
the selection of candidate officers by the royal academies in earlier
centuries. Nowadays the commitment and loyalty of the military
elite has to be transferred within the space of a few months, or even
weeks, and the new regime is sometimes quite different from the old
one.

The new political system will attempt to integrate the military
along different lines. Firstly, it will set out to change the system of
recruitment, promotion and discharge, retaining the most reliable
members of the forces and at the same time recruiting new members
from the most loyal milieus.

Secondly, a policy of indoctrination and political education introduces the new political formula, and is at the same time intended
to suppress any remaining feelings of loyalty toward the former sys-

tem. Besides allocation and socialization techniques there is, thirdly, the direct organizational control of the armed forces by the political system, by party leaders and political commissars.

This chapter is an attempt to examine the political control of the military in times of rapid political change. It deals first with the accumulated results of research as reported in this volume.

There are two general questions to be answered: (1) under what conditions do the new authorities succeed in gaining a firm control of the military institution; and (2) what circumstances cause a gradual erosion of the political pressure after that control has been established, and a return to greater professional autonomy, or even to military intervention in the political sphere?

FINDINGS

Establishing the new army.—The emergence of a completely new political order may raise the fundamental question of whether armed forces are in fact either necessary or useful.

The Soviet Union, as an orthodox communist system, started by abolishing the regular army. The new leaders made attempts to replace it by arming the people who were to be supported by strong international forces, but gradually returned to a regular army, general conscription and, finally, to absorption of the national military traditions.

Next to this famous experiment may be placed the plan to abdicate sovereignty in military affairs by accepting a United Nations Trusteeship, as did Tanzania in its first years of independence. But Mazrui shows clearly how this country developed in a few years into one of the most militant states of the African continent in response to internal unrest and the rise of African liberation movements.[2]

The USSR and Tanzania are exceptions. Normally, new political systems as well as new nations never question the formation of armed forces. In many cases the new regime emerges in the course of a military revolt, a civil war or a combination of civil and inter-state struggle. The Soviet Union, for instance had to fight a civil war complicated by the intervention of foreign powers. A better case in point is the emergence through military violence of People's China,

Korea, Indonesia, Algeria and Israel—*bien étonné de se trouver ensemble*. In other countries the new order was not the product of a liberation war, but was established after a long period of warfare, with the consequent necessity for a thorough reorganization of the armed forces.

In all these countries the newly-established army may be regarded as a fusion of a number of different military groups: regular troops, guerrilla bands, militia and mercenary forces, armed party units or militant religious movements. The first problem is the integration of these forces into a national army.

This process of organizational and normative fusion encounters tensions and resistance rooted in the recent historical events. In socialist countries the main challenge consists in the integration of military units with divergent ideological commitments. In most of the new states the first source of trouble is the regional heterogeneity of the troops, often a heritage of the highly selective recruitment policy of the colonial rulers.

If a strong enough nucleus force is available the fusion process has a good chance of succeeding (USSR, China, Israel). In many cases, however, the divergent origins of the troops create more of less dangerous tensions in the military establishment. It often takes a long time to establish a well-integrated armed force, as is shown in the case of North Korea by Jae Souk Sohn, and of some West-African nations by Zolberg.[3] Even after years, a collapse may occur. The civil war in Nigeria may be a horrifying illustration, but other new states have also had to contend with disastrous inter-army strains and conflicts. In Indonesia, for example, tension exploded in open conflict in 1955, touching off a civil war which lasted over three years and was supported by regional interests.[4]

Warned by clashes like these, many new states have strong feelings about regional controversies which sometimes develop into a full-fledged "civil war complex," as in Tanzania. The military leaders make serious efforts to broaden the recruitment base of the forces in accordance with the idea of the army functioning as a nation-building institution.

To generalize, it may be hypothesized that the socialist countries usually succeed in the integration of the armed forces, while many new nations suffer from inter-army tensions which sometimes give rise to a succession of military interventions supported by a changing variety of army branches and local commanders.

Purging the old forces.—New regimes often cannot do without the military forces on hand at the moment of power transfer. In these cases where the new political order happened to be established in a short time and under relatively peaceful conditions, the new army has to make a start with the old personnel. But even a process of violent revolution and civil war leaves the new rulers with a great number of field officers and military specialists from the old regime.

Soviet Union. The Red Army needed its Tsarist officers right from the beginning. Some 25,000 former officers were conscripted as early as 1918, and during the whole of the civil war between 50,000 and 100,000 officers of the Imperial Army were absorbed into the Red Army.[5]

Poland. In 1949 18% of all officers were pre-war professionals, and were used mostly as experts.[6]

Czechoslovakia. In 1952, 17.6% of the officers had belonged to the corps before 1945.

Many of these older officers play a very important role and are especially numerous in the higher ranks. Even around 1930, the old officers still dominated military thinking in the Soviet Union.[7]

In the new states another heritage has to be accepted: ex-colonial officers and Western-trained men. In Asian countries the "Indianization" of the officer had made considerable progress before independence, but the "Africanization" of the colonial officer corps started late, in fact no more than a decade before independence.

Inevitably, many new nations had to retain parts of their Western officer corps and, after a gradual process of replacement, to accept long-planned military assistance such as the employment of some thousands of English, French and Soviet officers and NCOs, and the training facilities for their own new cadres provided by the United States, West- and East-European countries.

The self-esteem of the new regimes—and sometimes their self-protection—make a gradual purge of the old officer corps imperative. While the Soviet Union did not succeed in creating a fully professional as well as proletarian army before the thirties, the socialist countries of the second generation moved somewhat faster in recruiting new officers and discharging those they replaced. By 1967 the 17.6% of the old Czechoslovakian officers in 1952 had dwindled to 2.2%,[8] a trend which will also be found in the other East-European countries.

This development is, in the new states, clearly apparent in Africa, where the process of Africanization is now almost entirely complete. The last British officers were replaced in 1961 in Ghana, in 1965 in Nigeria, and in 1964 in Uganda and Tanzania.[9]

The creation of a new officers corps does not necessarily imply its political control. Ways and means of achieving this kind of control will now be considered.

Control by recruitment and selection.—What may be termed "Africanization" and "Indianization" in the new states is planned "proletarization" under communist rule. Some once-aristocratic officer corps, in particular, have undergone a fundamental change in social composition. In mid-nineteenth century Russia the majority of the officers were the sons of nobles, in 1930, or thereabouts, 25% of the officer corps were from a working-class background, and more than 50% from a peasant background.[10] A similar situation obtains in respect of the Imperial German Army compared with the *Volksarmee* of the DDR.

A striking point here is the way in which the aristocratic older control mechanisms devised to make the officer corps socially homogeneous have been adopted to serve the process of proletarization. In pre-war Poland an officer was not supposed to marry a woman of lower status, and a President's Order (1937) stated that anyone disobeying this order might be dismissed from the services. In post-war Poland officers were officially encouraged to marry into the workers and poor peasants classes.[11]

The move toward the proletarization of the Soviet Army has in fact been much more slow than in the post-World War II socialist countries (see Table 1).

In the Western countries a gradual influx of workers' sons in the officer corps has also taken place, influenced inter alia by the broadening of recruitment in World War II. But this process of "democratization" cannot be described as a well-planned policy of the government. In the socialist countries this policy had to guarantee the loyalty to the new regime.

Table 1.   Social Origin of Officers in Three Socialist Countries (in percentages)[12]

	Workers	Farmers	Others	Total
DDR (1965)	82.2	2.6	15.2	100
CSSR (1967)	60.8	12.7	26.5	100
Poland (1964)	47.7	33.4	18.9	100

Another measure designed to obtain the same result is the promotion of NCOs stimulated by the new socialist regimes. In 1952, 30.3% of all Czech officers were former NCOs.

Inevitably, this promotion policy providing new channels for upward social mobility radically lowered the level of education, both higher as well as military education. The authors describing the situation in the DDR, Czechoslovakia and Poland agree that in the first period of army construction the criterion of political loyalty weighed more heavily than that of professional ability.[13]

DDR. In 1956, only 0.2% of all officers had attended a military college. One out of every 55 had reached the level of higher education at a university or technical college.

Czechoslovakia. In 1957, 55% of the candidates accepted as officers had not completed their secondary education.

Poland. In the first period of the Polish People's Army most of its officers had no secondary education whatsoever.

It is probable that this lower educational level was in some way responsible for the notably low social prestige of officers in those countries, as is demonstrated in the case of Poland by Wiatr.[14]

Another symptom corresponding with the break in the military institutions of the socialist countries is the complete absence of self-recruitment. In many other countries (USA, Great Britain, France, Western Germany, Holland) the percentage of officers from officers' families is rather high (10-40%), thus demonstrating the cohesiveness and closeness of military professionalism.[15]

Very few data on the new states are available. The general picture, however, does not suggest a selective recruitment policy but a radical change, both regionally and socially, in the recruitment methods followed by the former colonial governments.[16] The new-nation officers are generally of middle class or lower class origin, and an army career offers attractive educational opportunities which can also be put to use in civil occupations.

The most serious danger recognized by the new regimes is regional recruitment, which can create tensions in the armed forces and, in consequence of this, in the political system as such. The de-tribalization and nationalization of the officer corps is the main issue as far as the new states are concerned, and not selective recruitment in accordance with a special political system.

The armed forces of the new states have to this extent a latent or manifest function in the process of nation-building. That function is of special importance in the case of nations faced with the necessity to integrate large numbers of immigrants from abroad. Israel is a famous and recent example of this policy.

Control by indoctrination.—A second mechanism designed to ensure loyalty of the military to the new regime is a policy of indoc-trination.

In socialist states—as well as in fascist ones—there is open agreement on the self-evidency of the full politicization of the armed forces. Being one-party systems, membership of the party is con-sidered to be the most effective way of guaranteeing the political commitment of the officer. The first decade of regimes of this kind consequently shows a gradual increase in the party membership of military professionals. It is interesting to compare the fast politic-ization of the military in the new socialist states with the more gradual process in the Soviet Union.[17]

A key institution in this process is the military academy, where much time is devoted to political studies, in complete contrast to the system of professional socialization in Western armed forces. The indoctrination process is intensified during the period of active service, often by special campaigns.

The whole program of systematic and enduring politicization is aimed at the creation of a military officer who is a professional expert as well as a politically active citizen. The two roles are con-sidered to be mutually supporting rather than being likely to cause personal and institutional tensions.

Consequently, ideological deviations will be rejected as a threat to the pursuit of institutional homogeneity and cohesion. Purges like those carried out in the Soviet Union in the thirties, in North Korea in the fifties and in Communist China in the sixties[18] are the drastic answer to this threat. It is beyond the scope of this chapter to include similar tendencies in fascist countries, especially in Germany (1933-1945), where gradual politicization was attempted, initially by the party, and later with the full support of the *Oberbefehlshaber.*

The non-European new states seldom attempt this sort of party indoctrination of the armed forces. On the contrary, the colonial tradition of a neutral army is usually continued. Like other young nations, including those of earlier centuries, strong emphasis is placed on the national character of the military institution and on its socializing function for the younger generation (Israel, USA).

New states which institute a social and political "mobilization" movement of this kind may be expected to show the corresponding tendency to control the military by indoctrination.

Control by organization.—Two main patterns of civil-military relations are discernible in socialist countries. The armed forces are always distinctly subordinated to the party but the interrelation of party and army elite differs.

In some cases the combined political and military control is embodied in one group of leaders, who dominate both the party machine and the armed forces (Communist China, North Korea, North Vietnam).[19] Elites of this kind are a product of the revolutionary war, in contrast to the dualism in communist regimes which have come to power by an unexpected move or under relatively peaceful conditions. In such countries control of the armed forces is much more the outcome of the party's penetration of the military apparatus (USSR and other East-European countries). In any case, in both types of party-military relations all high-ranking officers belong to the party. The integration of party and army is further guaranteed by the wide participation of officers in party committees.

The most fundamental means of political control, however, is the dual system of military and political command extending right down to the lower echelons first developed in the Soviet Army and later adopted by a number of other socialist regimes. In this type of organization the army has its own Political Bureau, which is the power centre of the party inside the military establishment. It covers the ideological and political indoctrination at all levels of the military hierarchy. A key figure in this control system is the 'political commissar', who exercises direct party control on the commanding officers.

The chain of command from the highest to the lowest levels thus consists of two lines of control: one by the political party and one by the professional military.[20] Ironically, the German Army under National Socialism adopted this control system by creating the *N. S. Führungsoffiziere* (1943), whose task was a similar one.[21]

Within the broader framework of the political system as a whole, the formation of special party militias or military armed police forces introduces the same dualist structure on a larger scale. It is not only the individual officer who has a controlling party member at his side; the regular army as such also has to tolerate a rival organization. This dualistic policy may be expected to be particularly in evidence in those countries where the party is not fully confident of the conforming effect of selective recruitment and indoctrination of the officer corps.

Despite many differences between the new communist regimes and the new nations in Asia and Africa, there is some similarity in their organizational control pattern of the military. Dudley and Zolberg convincingly demonstrate the close relations between the political and the military elite in a number of new states.[22] As a consequence, there is no clear distinction or distance between the two institutions, as is the case in most Western countries.

This helps to explain the relatively undramatic political consequences of a take-over by the armed forces, but also the tendency of the military to occupy political positions to an extent unknown in Western political systems.

Yet the politicization of the armed forces is generally limited to strong nationalist sympathies and commitments, which are only occasionally overshadowed by ideological preferences.

There is nevertheless no reason to deny that the organizational control of the military is much weaker in the new states than in socialist countries. But in spite of the opportunity for the military to intervene, practically all new states began their existence under civilian rule and the majority have succeeded in maintaining this political order, often under difficult circumstances. The next question is what are their chances of survival in the coming decade.

Erosion of political control.—It is a general phenomenon that after a time new social systems have to contend with a certain measure of reaction; they are often challenged by a routinization of charisma of the leaders and by a decline in the élan and loyalty of the followers. Dysfunctional developments manifest themselves: oligarchic and bureaucratic structures come into existence which, ceasing to be an instrument of change, become instead one of its first obstacles.

It is to be expected that the political control pattern of the military will also be reshaped after the first period of one-sided domination by the political regime. The now firmly established system will be disposed to loosen its grip on the new situation, a situation which promotes moves to restructure the control mechanism. In concrete terms, the armed forces attempt to increase their autonomy within the newly-built political context.

In the material available there are a number of indications in support of this hypothesis. Some of the authors refer to the existence of two periods—revolutionary and post-revolutionary, but their analysis offers an even greater opportunity to make such a distinction in the course of events.

The general trend may be defined as the gradual restoration of professional criteria. In the recruitment of officers the level of education becomes a decisive factor, in contrast to the first period when political liability was the dominant criterion.

DDR. The extraordinarily small percentage of officers with an adequate military education—0.2% in 1956—rose to 77% by 1965 for the category of regimental and divisional commanders.[23]

CSSR. In 1951 only 8% of all officers had graduated from a military academy; in 1966 the figure was 28%.[24]

Poland. According to Graczyk, the phase of below-standard education was followed by serious efforts to intensify the officers' training program. The situation is now such that the proportion of officers with a higher education (23.9% by the end of 1964) far exceeds the corresponding category in other professional sectors.[25]

USSR. After a period of struggle between the "proletarians" and the military specialists, the professionalization of the officer corps was started in earnest about 1930. At present, nine out of ten officers have a higher or secondary education qualification.[26]

People's China. Military professionalism was accepted with the adoption of the "Regulations on the Service of Officers" in February 1955, and regular channels for entry and promotion have been firmly established.[27]

Another trend indicating the same weakening of purely political standards is the broadening of the social recruitment base. Zhilin's general statement about the Soviet Union—"the class principle of military construction was applied on a temporary basis"[28]—may have value for some other socialist countries as well. In analyzing Table 2, the influence of the changing occupational structure on the recruitment pattern should be borne in mind.

Table 2.   Trends in the Social Origin of Officers in Some Socialist Countries (in percentages)[29]

		1952	1957	1962	1967
CSSR	Workers	53.8	63.3	63.5	60.8
	Farmers	13.9	12.9	12.4	12.7
	Intelligentsia	15.3	11.8	13.1	16.1
	Others	17.0	12.0	11.0	10.4
	Total	100	100	100	100
		1958	1962	1964	
Poland	Workers	51.0	48.6	47.7	
	Farmers	34.1	33.3	33.4	
	Intelligentsia	10.3	11.3	12.2	
	Others	4.6	6.8	6.7	
	Total	100	100	100	

These figures which suggest the end of the "proletarization" process of the officer corps, find clear support in the material relating to the social origin of the younger military generation in Poland presented by Graczyk.[30] In the years 1958-64 about 50% of all officers came from workers' families, though in the same period only some 40% of the candidates for officers' colleges were the sons of workers. The figures giving the proportion of intelligentsia show the reverse: about 10% and 20% respectively.

This pattern is also demonstrated by the modest but unmistakable process of self-recruitment adopted in Czechoslovakia. In the Soviet Union it was even formally stimulated from above.

These processes may explain the gradual rise of social prestige after a period when it was at a very low ebb and the relatively high social standing of the military in the Soviet Union.[31]

The restoration of military professionalism indicated above does not correlate with the development of party membership among officers. The proportion is either very high and stable or it goes on growing.

It is not the bare fact of membership which is decisive, however, but its ideological control function. It seems probable that this function has weakened since the first period. Party affiliation is first and foremost a prerequisite for promotion, not an expression of strong orthodox feelings.[32]

Where a post-revolutionary generation of young officers trained in professional institutions and working in their own rather isolated milieu starts to dominate the officer corps, their political commitment is likely to lose part of its control function. Contradictions occur between political and professional requirement and interests and lead either to covert strains (Soviet Union)[33] or to open conflict (People's China).[34]

Burning issues may include the strategic doctrines—weapons or men—military leadership—one-man command—and the degree of direct political influence in professional socialization. The armed forces are inclined to stress their own criteria and preferences, even in opposition to the political leaders, if necessary.

This situation repeatedly provokes indoctrination campaigns, the reinforcement of political loyalty and, under some circumstances, purges, or at least the replacement of popular military leaders.

In conclusion, it may be pointed out that the first period of tight political control of the military is often followed by a second phase characterized by disputes between the political and military leaders arising out of their division of labor and interests.

Distinguishing between the two periods requires concrete

knowledge about the multitude of factors influencing the evolution of civil-military relations in a given nation; war experience, international tensions, technological level and inner-party power shifts may be of importance.

Emerging military intervention.—In socialist and other totalitarian systems the political control of the military may be disputed after a time, but it is seldom seriously endangered. In new nations, however, the danger of military intervention is, on the evidence, very great.

Nevertheless, it is exceptional for a take-over by the military to follow immediately on the proclamation of national independence. Almost all new nations start with civilian governments. Erosion of the newly-established political structure, however, occurs much faster and more dramatically than in the new socialist states, which heightens the chance of complete collapse at the moment of military pressure.

One could perhaps say that the second period of rule mentioned above is characterized in new states by the open confrontation of political and military power. If the outcome of this struggle is in many cases a take-over of the regime by the armed forces, the explanation is to be found in the failure to build up a political control structure like that maintained by socialist regimes.

Since our knowledge of military intervention in new states is drawn from a mass of empirical evidence, no further presentation of data is necessary. What does require some further explanation, however, is the difference between socialist and new states.

DISCUSSION

The problem tentatively investigated in this essay may be defined as the ability of the political elite to control the armed forces despite a process of radical political change. The results demonstrate first of all that in both socialist and other new states the necessity to establish a new political order strong enough to dominate the armed forces constitutes a serious challenge.

Secondly, both types of new regime meet this challenge in quite distinctive ways. Thirdly, the confrontation of political and military power would seem to lead to a different outcome, since the socialist states succeed in their control policy while the regimes of the new nations often break down under the pressure of military intervention.

It is necessary to discuss the problem along two separate lines before attempting an interpretation of these differences. First, one must ask whether the character of the political control can explain the difference; second, one must examine the various types of armed forces in their relation to politics.

The structuring of political control.—As Finer suggests, the probability of military intervention is related to the level of what he calls "political culture."[35] When that level is high, the pressure from the military has only very restricted consequences; when it is low, the replacement of the civil authorities by military leaders, or at least their manipulation of the government, can be expected.

This theory is applicable to the problem under discussion. A point of similarity between a number of new communist and the new nationalist regimes is the existence of an initially low political culture: the center of power, if any, lacks full legitimacy, the effectiveness of the government administration is poor, the transfer of power is not yet institutionalized, and the civic institutions have still to find their place in the new political order and in public approval.

From the analysis of Dudley and Zolberg and of other experts it may be concluded that many new nations suffer from an inherent political instability. On the one hand the new super-structure has but weak roots in the old tribal and peasant society; on the other hand there is only a very restrictive modern societal and political structure (associations, unions, parties). The transformation of the authoritarian colonial rule into a more or less democratic system therefore takes place under unfavorable conditions.

The resulting low degree of legitimacy and effectiveness of the new government makes it difficult for it to survive any decisive move of the military in political affairs. In some African countries mutinies could only be suppressed with the aid of foreign troops (in Congo-Kinshasa by UN-Forces, in Tanzania by British forces), while in many other states the weak civilian government was after a time completely overruled by the military.

The impressive number of recent military coups in new states emphasizes the fact that no such intervention occurs in new communist states. Some comparative cases, like North and South Korea, or North and South Vietnam, seem to prove that it is not exactly the level of political culture but the political ideology which is decisive in civil-military relations.

The essays of Sohn on North Korea and of Mazrui on Tanzania[36] give the impression, however, that ideology is not a sufficient explanation. What characterizes both countries is the systematic construction of a political organization throughout society, including a one-party system, mobilization of the masses, youth movements, and the direct control of the military by the party. The differences between both countries, though immense, are only in degree, not in principle.

The planned political structuring of society seems to form the first principal protection against military intervention; it is the 'filling up' of the power vacuum. From this point of view the successful socialist control of the armed forces is not, or not in the first place, the result of indoctrination, but is founded on a strong complex of organizational and institutional controls. It can be successful in countries with either a higher or a lower political culture, because the policy of the new regime succeeds in realizing some of the institutional prerequisites of a higher political culture in a very short space of time.

It is an open question, however, to what extent a non-communist system may be able to create such a new political order. The destruction of the Peronist regime in Argentina by a military oligarchy and the successful military take-over in Ghana suggest that even an authoritarian mass-party system can be overruled.[32]

It may be concluded that the forced build-up of political controls in a process of rapid change strong enough to keep the military in its subservient position presupposes the existence of a political elite with sufficient insight, radicalism and resources to build up comparatively swiftly an all-pervasive structure of societal and political institutions and power positions, mutually interconnected and centralized at the top in one party.

The autonomy of the military profession.—The second question is whether the survival of a new regime can be explained by a high degree of military professionalism. Huntington points out that only a highly professional officer corps is willing to accept full control of the civilian government.[38]

Huntington's theory seems to find support in the experience of most modern democratic countries since the officer corps in those countries is highly professionalized and at the same time not disposed to intervene in politics. In fact, the military take up a politically "neutral" position, and are prepared to redefine their role in the context of their profession.

Lang's analysis of the abortive coups in Germany in 1944 and in France in 1961 provides new support for Huntington's idea that a highly professional army is a highly a-political one. It was partly their professional outlook and their traditional distaste for politics which hindered a successful putsch, even in moments of complete desperation.

> An army in whose tradition the principle of obedience to civil authority has been raised to an absolute principle cannot at the same time include an equally compelling structural imperative to engage in a *coup d'état*. . . . Even those who ultimately became the prime movers for a coup went through long soul-searching to find a justification.[39]

The military profession being an instrument of the government, it is of course not without interest in politics. International developments are followed with special attention and continually influence strategic insights and preferences. It is also true that the military educational system selects and indoctrinates the *Nachwuchs*. Generally speaking, however, this is all primarily a professional affair. The criteria used, the values indoctrinated and the beliefs and the outlook adopted largely serve the performance of the professional task within the framework of a given political order.

The question is now whether we are right in supposing that where military professionalism is high there will be no difficulty in maintaining political control of the military in the event of rapid political change.

The fascist "revolution" in Germany in 1933 and the communist coup in Czechoslovakia in 1948, whereby the change of political system was effected both swiftly and relatively peacefully, confirm that supposition. On the two occasions in question there was an almost complete lack of resistance on the part of the armed forces, despite the radical break in the political order. Even stronger confirmation seems to be provided by the high degree of subservience displayed by the German officer corps some decades earlier, when *der Kaiser* was replaced by a socialist government. Despite serious doubts in military circles there was general obedience.

One can go a step further and claim that even the Soviet Army, influenced as it has been for half a century by a continual bombardment of ideological orthodoxy, prefers an a-political identity. Kolkowicz's analysis of the tensions between the political and the professional role in the Soviet officer corps leads to the conclusion that professionalism is succeeding in restraining political influence and in gaining greater professional autonomy.[40]

It may be concluded that the reprofessionalization of the military in the post-revolutionary period, as described above, will not really endanger the political control pattern *unless* the political culture is low.

This is precisely the situation in those new states which have no sufficiently developed political structure as a heritage of pre-independence, or have been unable to build up such a structure in the first years of independence. In such countries, military professionalism, rather than constituting a mainstay of order, is a time bomb without a prearranged moment of explosion.

CONCLUSIONS

An analysis of political breaking points in history may provide greater insight into the power of a given regime to control the military.

Firstly, it seems to be necessary to make a clear distinction between socialist and other totalitarian political systems, and non-totalitarian new states. The former generally succeed in gaining and maintaining a firm grip on the armed forces, while many of the other categories lose that control after a time.

Secondly, this difference does not so much refer to a different "level of political culture" but to the ability of the successful regimes to build up in a very short space of time a complex of institutional controls throughout the social system, including the military sphere of power.

Thirdly, this success is more attributable to organizational control than to ideological indoctrination, since the socialist, fascist and other types of authoritarian mass party systems prove to have a tighter grip on the military than do other political systems.

The adoption of military professionalism, which is beneficial to highly developed political systems, seems to represent a danger to weak regimes, as is the case in many new nations outside Europe.

These tentative conclusions suggest a need for a reformulation of both Finer's and Huntington's hypotheses. It is not a low political culture as such that permits military intervention, but the impotence of the regime to safeguard the political order by a rapidly constructed pattern of organizational and other controls. Nor is it professionalization as such that prevents military intervention in politics, but the existence of a deep-rooted tradition of military detachment as well as the existence of a pattern of political control.

NOTES

[1]S. E. Finer, *The Man on Horseback: The Role of the Military in Politics* (London and Dunmow: Pall Mall Press, 1962), 86-89.

[2]Ali A. Mazrui, 'Anti-Militarism and Political Militancy in Tanzania', in Jacques van Doorn (ed.), *Military Profession and Military Regimes* (The Hague and Paris: Mouton, 1969), 219 ff.

[3]Jae Souk Sohn, 'Factionalism and Party Control of the Military in Communist North Korea', in Jacques van Doorn (ed.), *op. cit.*, 269 ff.; Aristide R. Zolberg, 'Military Rule and Political Development in Tropical Africa; A Preliminary Report', in *ibidem*, 157 ff.

[4]Guy J. Pauker, 'The Role of the Military in Indonesia', in John J. Johnson (ed.), *The Role of the Military in Underdeveloped Countries* (Princeton, N.J.: Princeton University Press, 1962), 211-13.

[5]Raymond L. Garthoff, 'The Military in Russia, 1861-1965', in Jacques van Doorn (ed.), *Armed Forces and Society* (The Hague and Paris: Mouton, 1968), 246.

[6]Jerzy J. Wiatr, 'Military Professionalism and Transformation of Class Structure in Poland', in Jacques van Doorn (ed.), *Armed Forces . . . , op. cit.,* 238.

[7]Jaromir Cvrcek, 'Social Changes in the Officer Corps of the Czechoslovak People's Army', in Jacques van Doorn (ed.), *Military Profession . . . , op. cit.,* 97; Garthoff, *op. cit.*, 247.

[8]Cvrcek, *op. cit.,* 97.

[9]M. J. V. Bell, 'The Military in the New States of Africa', in Jacques van Doorn (ed.), *Armed Forces . . . , op. cit.,* 261.

[10]Garthoff, *op. cit.,* 247.

[11]Wiatr, *op. cit.,* 234 f.

[12]For DDR: Erwin Stüber, Günter Rau and Karl-Heinz Schulze, 'The Problem of Militarism and the Armies of the Two German States', *Paper* presented at the 6th World Congress of Sociology, Evian (September 1966), 30; for CSSR: Crvcek, *op. cit.,* 97; for Poland: Józef Graczyk, 'Social Promotion in the Polish People's Army', in Jacques van Doorn (ed.), *Military Profession . . . , op. cit.,* 88.

[13]Stüber, Rau and Schulze, *op. cit.,* 32 ff.; Wiatr, *op. cit.,* 238; Crycek, *op. cit.,* 99.

[14]Wiatr, *op. cit.,* 236: 'The position of the officer was lowered in the process of expansion of the national economy, when other—industrial—professions became the most popular. Even more, the easy access to these professions made them less prestigious. . . .'

[15]USA and Germany: Morris Janowitz, *The Professional Soldier* (Ill: The Free Press of Glencoe, 1960), 96; Great Britain: C. B. Otley, 'Militarism and the Social Affiliations of the British Army Elite', in Jacques van Doorn (ed.), *Armed Forces . . . , op. cit.,* 90, 93; France: Raoul Girardet (ed.), *La crise militaire française, 1945-1962* (Paris: Armand Colin, 1964), 233; Holland: Jacques van Doorn, 'The Officer Corps: A Fusion of Profession and Organization', *Archives Européennes de Sociologie*, Vol. VI (1965), 279.

[16]Morris Janowitz, *The Military in the Political Process of New Nations* (Chicago and London: The University of Chicago Press, 1964), 49 ff., 52 f.

[17]DDR: Stüber, Rau and Schulze, *op. cit.*, 34; CSSR: Cvrcek, *op. cit.*, 96, 101; Garthoff, *op. cit.*, 247-53.

[18]Roman Kolkowicz, *The Soviet Military and the Communist Party* (Princeton, N.J.: Princeton U.P., 1967), 55 ff., 81 ff.; Sohn, *op. cit.*, 275 ff.; Ellis Joffe, *Party and Army: Professionalism and Political Control in the Chinese Officer Corps, 1949-1964* (Cambridge, Mass.: Harvard U.P., 1965), 47, 114 ff.

[19]Joffe, *op. cit.*, 44: 'Throughout the revolutionary period and for several years after 1949, there was little to distinguish the political from the military leaders. . . . The political and military commands were inextricably intertwined, and their tasks and experience were identical to a great extent.' Sohn, *op. cit.*, 271: 'Today the former anti-Japanese guerillas, who fought with Kim Il-sung, form the central axis not only of the army but of the party as well.'

[20]Garthoff, *op. cit.*, 248 ff.; Joffe, *op. cit.*, 58 ff.; I. Gadourek, *The Political Control of Czechoslovakia* (Leyden: Stenfert Kroese, 1953), 74 f.; Sohn, *op. cit.*, gives a detailed description of this system in the North Korean Army.

[21]*Offiziere im Bild von Dokumenten aus drei Jahrhunderten,* Hrg. Hans Meier-Welcker (Stuttgart: Deutsche Verlags-Anstalt, 1964), 104.

[22]B. J. Dudley, 'The Military and Politics in Nigeria: Some Reflections', in Jacques van Doorn (ed.), *Military Profession . . . , op. cit.*, 205 ff.; Zolberg, *op. cit.*, 198 f.

[23]Stüber, Rau and Schulze, *op. cit.*, 33.

[24]Cvrcek, *op. cit.*, 100.

[25]Graczyk, *op. cit.*, 91.

[26]P. Zhilin, 'The Armed Forces of the Soviet Union', in Jacques van Doorn (ed.), *Military Profession . . . , op. cit.*, 167.

[27]Joffe, *op. cit.*, 30-36.

[28]Zhilin, *op. cit.*, 171.

[29]CSSR: Cvrcek, *op. cit.*, 97; Poland: Graczyk, *op. cit.*, 88.

[30]Graczyk, *op. cit.*, 89.

[31]Garthoff, *op. cit.*, 255 f.

[32]Garthoff, *op. cit.*, 253.

[33]Kolkowicz, *op. cit.*, parts II and III.

[34]Joffe, *op. cit.*, ch. 2.

[35]Finer, *op. cit.*, 87 ff.

[36]Mazrui, *op. cit.*

[37]The case of Ghana is not conclusive since the regime seemed much less firmly established than had been suggested by its image. 'Nkrumah lacked the imagination and skill to develop a country. He was a revolutionary without a plan—a visionary, but not a builder.' David E. Apter, 'Nkrumah, Charisma, and the Coup', *Daedalus,* Vol. 97 (Summer 1968), 788.

[38]Samuel P. Huntington, *The Soldier and the State: The Theory and Politics of Civil-Military Relations* (Cambridge, Mass.: Harvard U.P., 1957), 83 f.

[39]Kurt Lang, 'The Military Putsch in a Developed Political Culture: Confrontations of Military and Civil Power in Germany and France', in Jacques van Doorn (ed.), *Armed Forces . . . , op. cit.*, 217, 227 f.

[40]Kolkowicz, *op. cit.*

Chapter 5

THE MILITARY AND THE CRISIS OF LEGITIMACY

INTRODUCTION

*A*s a discipline focused on a specific social institution, the sociology of the military constitutes a collection of divergent subjects, such as morale and leadership, small groups, formal organization and professionalism, social origin and military intervention. The principal difficulty is that the entire field of study is too fragmentary and disjointed, and it is partly for this reason that discussion of its various aspects is often highly descriptive and relates to only one particular geographical region. There is no close tie with either the quintessential problems of sociology or the major sociological theories. With the exception of the social origins of the officer corps, little cumulative research has been undertaken, and in fact much of what is carried out amounts to argumentation of the body of empirical knowledge with no further theoretical processing.

A modest opportunity to arrive at a general analysis is presented by the present crisis of legitimacy. This term implies a comprehensive complex of developments, such as the diminishing acceptance of military force, the increasing public criticism of the military, the popularity of compulsory military service, the decivilianization of the military and the concomitant loss of institutional identity. Though these phenomena are especially evident in the Western developed countries, they are also found in the socialist world while, moreover, the role of the military is a controversial issue in the developing countries, not least because of its intervention in politics.

These problems play a part in the external relations with the community and within the military organization itself. They are connected not only with civil-military relations but also with the changed forms of military violence which have given rise to dangerous technological advances and have at the same time to compete with guerilla warfare and civil defence.

One of the principal advantages of the study of this complex of phenomena is the fact that it presents possibilities in both the theoretical and the applied fields. The concept of legitimacy and its analytical potential opens up avenues for a more theoretical type of study, while the results of such an analysis provide points of departure for implementing and amending defence policy, organizational development and military education.

This chapter deals first with the conceptualization associated with the phenomenon of legitimacy, both as regards its general substance and the way it is usually classified; then with the problems of the military classed under the headings of the relations between the armed forces and the political order; and the armed forces and the use of violence.

CONCEPTUAL CLARIFICATION

Legitimacy and Related Concepts

What the term "legitimacy" is intended to convey can often be described in another way. David C. Rapoport's doctoral thesis, for instance, entitled *Praetorianism: Government without Consensus,* and later published under the title of *Praetorianism: Government without Authority,*[1] could just as easily have made use of the word "legitimacy". For the three terms "consensus", "authority" and "legitimacy" are all intended to convey the fact that the military establishment plays a dominating role without sufficient public support and political trust. Other terms with a meaning similar to that of legitimacy are authority and authoritativeness, political allegiance and political myth, compliance, justification and ideology, political culture, civic culture and civic competence. They all indicate in one way or another a normative approach to the political order and its incumbents or, more generally, to power structures within social systems.

There are invariably two parties, one claiming legitimacy in the sense of the right to exercise authority, to call for sacrifices and to receive recognition, and the other accepting this right and showing its readiness to accord recognition to the other's legitimate claims. Legitimacy thus includes both a normative and an evaluative orientation. This, however, is not enough. The party demanding legitimacy must also possess the requisite capacities, while the dependent party must show by its actions or its support that recognition is more than simply paying lip service to the idea.

Though the concept of legitimacy has a long history, especially in the field of constitutional law,[2] it was Max Weber who introduced it definitely into sociology in his major work, *Wirtschaft und Gesellschaft*,[3] though at first it remained very much restricted to the sphere of the political order, as is evident from various authoritative definitions. Sternberger, for instance, states that "legitimacy is the foundation of such governmental power as is exercised both with the consciousness on the government's part that it has a right to govern and with some recognition by the governed of that right."[4] Easton emphasizes the role of the politically dependent, perceiving in legitimacy a reflection "in some vague or explicit way" of the fact that a member of a political system is of the opinion that this system functions in accordance with "his own moral principles, his own sense of what is right and proper in the political sphere."[5] Lipset, while taking much the same view, defines legitimacy as an achievement of the political system itself: "The capacity of the system to engender and maintain the belief that the existing political institutions are the most appropriate ones for the society."[6]

A further definition now in vogue relates at most to the regular social order,[7] with which it is sometimes even quite unconnected in coinciding completely with a general readiness to accept the use of power within a system of institutionalized expectations regarding the exercise of authority.[8] Ball-Rokeach stretches her definition to extremes in simply regarding legitimacy as "a collective judgement that attributes the qualities of 'goodness' or 'morality' or 'righteousness' to behavior."[9]

Our own definition is a variant of that of Lipset. It is wider than that restricted to the political scene, but narrower than that which is applicable to every kind of social behavior and is therefore identical to authority. In our view, *legitimacy is the capacity of a social or political system to develop and maintain a general belief that the existing social order and its main institutions are generally appropriate.*

(1) It concerns a *system variable,* not the ability of an individual, in which case it would be better to speak in terms of loyalty or trust.

(2) It relates to the *capacity* of a system, and not to a given situation. The system is not automatically endowed with legitimacy, but achieves it through its actions.[10]

(3) As regards the words *"generally* appropriate," the qualitative and quantitative support are matters for further research.[11]

Some Classifications

All forms of legitimacy have their place within a system of levels, each being a generalization of attitudes at the previous level.[12] The three main levels are:

(1) the social or political order, usually embodied in an elite or regime. In many cases the legitimacy is elaborated in a doctrine explicitly justifying the existing order. Political ideologies and myths are examples of such doctrines;

(2) institutions or formal organizations, insofar as—Parsons states[13]—they are part of a wider social system in which their role has to be legitimized. This happens if the value system of the organization or institution is recognized within the framework of the generalized values of the superordinate system. Articulation of these values devolves upon the highest (political or institutional) level of the organization;

(3) social roles incorporating authority derived from either the social or political order as a whole (the policeman) or the position occupied by the person concerned in a formal organization

(the foreman). It should be noted that this micro concept of legitimate power is not far removed from the outer limits of what legitimacy constitutes. In such cases we usually speak in terms of authority and loyalty in general. The authority holder may, however, authorize his actions by specific reference to his legitimate rights.

The legitimacy of social institutions, organizations and roles is a derived, or reflected, legitimacy. It is important to take note of this, for a strengthening or weakening of 'lower level' legitimacy will have consequences for that at the higher levels, and vice versa. To give a specific example, any weakening of the legitimacy of the political regime impedes the day-to-day activities of the policeman; conversely, indecisive action on the part of the police undermines the feelings of legitimacy towards the government.

Weber's contribution is not so much his analysis of legitimacy in general as the distinction he makes between rational-legal, traditional and charismatic sources of legitimacy. By constructing these ideal types he was able to distinguish between various types of legitimate social order and to fashion an instrument for the analysis of the transformation of types of legitimacy. He makes it clear that we are dealing with the general characteristics of the social and political order. The sources of legitimacy are part of a certain political culture and are an expression of a social climate. This being the case, legitimacy cannot be "proclaimed" or "imposed" but must take shape in the course of a historical process in which the authority actually exercised is of crucial importance. As Nettl states in his study of developing countries, "before legitimacy can be ratified, it must exist; before authority can become legitimate, it must be or at one time have been effective and must be recognized as such."[14]

We should thus distinguish between legitimacy as a state of affairs and legitimation as a process. It follows from this that the complementary concepts are "illegitimacy" for the lack of legitimacy, and "delegitimation" for the disappearance of legitimacy.

Legitimacy as a Potentiality

The remarkable thing about legitimacy is its association with social relations rooted in basic premises which mean that power-holders can make decisions without having to wait to see whether they will be accepted for they can generally rely upon their being accepted. The power subjects do not examine each decision separately; they do not obey because they are convinced of the rightness of a certain decision but because they recognize the right of the power holders to make this and similar decisions. The two elements involved here are not personal responsibility and personal motivation, but generalized rights and recognition of those rights.[15]

Etzioni[16] observes rightly that support should not be confused with satisfaction. He points out that army officers who lead their men in battle have the right to do so, but the fact that this right is recognized by the men does not mean that they consider it preferable to fight. Soldiers do not separately assess each decision of their commanding officer because they recognize his leadership as legitimate and, moreover, have confidence in his powers of leadership. The latter is the psychological complement of legitimate military leadership. Easton, who defines legitimacy as "support," therefore rightly refers to "diffuse support" as separate from the daily output of the political system. This creates as it were a reservoir of positive attitudes which are not dissimilar to phenomena such as goodwill and loyalty.[17]

Homans, without referring explicitly to legitimacy, uses the term "capital" to indicate the possibility of postponing actions leading to immediate rewards.

> The capital may take the form of unusually well-disciplined soldiers; it may take the form of a surplus of food or money; most important of all, it may take the form of a moral code, especially a code supporting trust and confidence between men. . . .[18]

These definitions make it easier to place the concept of legitimacy.

The concept of institutionalization is the core of the matter. The function of institutionalization is to be found in the "economy of consensus,"[19] which derives its value from the fact that the processing capacity of social systems is limited. In hierarchical relations this takes the form of trust and loyalty. Power becomes authority, which is to say that the exercise of power is accepted on the basis of consensus. The process of the exercise of power is thus counterbalanced by the process of the acceptance of authority. But this is not yet legitimate power, for the acceptance of authority may be based on nothing more than custom and habit, on apathetic resignation to the existing social inequality. Legitimacy only enters into the picture when inequality is found to be justified on the basis of generalized societal values or, in other words, when inequality fits into the framework of a certain social order.

The need for legitimate social order of this kind becomes more pressing as the social division of labor advances. The social and political systems then become too complex for the simple, individual acceptance of decisions, necessitating the creation of a legitimate order in which decisions of all kinds can be made even if those concerned are not in possession of all details and are not fully convinced.[20] It follows from this that the legitimacy of a social system cannot be measured in terms of exact majorities and minorities, as with elections. Legitimacy is not founded on, or guaranteed by, 51% being in favor of a decision. It consists rather of fairly general support for certain institutions and of the absence of explicit and successful resistance to the continued existence of these institutions.

Once acceptance of the system is made dependent on the percentage of those voting in favor of certain decisions, legitimacy begins to disappear. It has to be measured against the existence of belief in a common political culture and in mechanisms and procedures guaranteeing that the system will function in conformity with this culture.

Legitimacy and Effectiveness

As noted earlier, a claim to legitimacy is not sufficient; effective channels and means must also be available and action must be undertaken for the confirmation and maintenance of that claim. Deutsch elaborates this thesis in his example of the failure of legitimate governments-in-exile in World War II when they were not in possession of actual networks of communication channels for two-way streams of information. This is indispensable.

> Without widespread and favorable legitimacy beliefs, a face-to-face communications network is exceedingly hard to build. . . . Without effective control of the bulk of the actual communication networks, on the other hand the nominal holders of the legitimacy symbols may become relatively helpless vis-à-vis those groups that do have this control.[21]

This brings us to the question of how the relation between legitimacy and the effectiveness of an elite should be viewed. There are various opinions on this.

Lipset is the most in favor of distinguishing between them. While he views legitimacy as evaluation, effectiveness for him amounts to actual performance, or:

> . . . the extent to which the system satisfies the basic functions of government as most of the population and such powerful groups within it as big business or the armed forces see it.[22]

He nevertheless perceives an interconnection, especially in the long term, in that prolonged effectiveness over a long period will give legitimacy to a political system. This tells us nothing, however, of the interconnection at the moment when it is determined that there is a belief in both the legitimacy and the effectiveness of the regime. For the effectiveness or efficiency will be evaluated and weighed by the population.[23]

We have the impression that Apter, for one, has drawn consequences from this in tracing legitimacy back to two types of values, which he terms consummatory and instrumental. The first is of a moral nature, while the second relates to appreciation of the degree of effectiveness with which a regime tackles problems.[24] Though this distinction is both valid and practicable, we nevertheless maintain that legitimacy and effectiveness can indeed be distinguished one from the other if we interpret Lipset consistently and place the first concept in the normative sphere and the second in the sphere of social action. Effectiveness can then be measured with the aid of a number of yardsticks, such as the output of the system, the allocation of resources, the degree of cohesion between its constituent parts and the ability to bring about some consent among its members.[25]

This should not be taken to mean that legitimacy and effectiveness can exist independently of each other. The extent of their interrelationship, however, and the explanation for it, are subjects for empirical research and do hardly lend themselves to theoretical reflection.

THE LEGITIMATE POLITICAL ORDER AND THE ARMED FORCES

Armed Forces as the Embodiment of a Legitimate Order

Huntington has observed that the form of government is less important than the degree of government as a distinguishing criterion.

> The differences between democracy and dictatorship are less than the differences between those countries whose politics embody consensus, community, legitimacy, organization, effectiveness, stability, and those countries whose politics are deficient in these qualities.[26]

This is equally applicable to the position and role of the armed forces: whether they form part of some superordinate legitimate order or are isolated and viewed with suspicion from that order. The difference between liberal and social democracies, right-wing and left-wing totalitarian systems, old and new states, is of secondary importance here.

It might be stated as a general rule of thumb that the legitimacy of the armed forces was guaranteed as long as: (1) the function of the military coincided sufficiently with what the political community defined as legitimate goals; (2) the military sub-culture coincided sufficiently with the political culture of the larger unit; and (3) the composition of the armed forces was sufficiently representative of the composition of the political community.

Limiting ourselves to the nineteenth and twentieth centuries, we can distinguish four types of civil-military relations in which the above requirements were met to such an extent that the armed forces were rightly regarded as the embodiment of the legitimate political order.

(1) The citizen army of the national revolutions, particularly those of the American and French Revolutions. The *levée en masse* spelled the end of the monopoly position of the aristocracy in the armed forces and the beginning of a close relationship between the political community and the military. In these revolutions the citizens seized power from the traditional, feudal

authorities and based their claims on a new source of legitimacy, popular sovereignty. The armed forces were the armed element of these political revolutions. It was this period that produced the right of the citizen to bear arms as an expression of his new status as a citizen.

(2)   The conscript army of the national state, particularly as it developed in nineteenth-century Prussia and was later copied by other continental nation states. Not the people but the state now became the source of legitimacy and the principal guarantee for the maintenance of that state was the national armed force based on compulsory military service. In this system conscription was more than learning to use weapons; it also provided an excellent means of learning the national virtues in the *Schule der Nation,* as the army was regarded, and of serving the state. The other social institutions, such as family, school and church, supported the legitimacy of the armed forces and contributed to recognition of its function.

(3)   The politicized army of the totalitarian regimes, both fascist and communist. The legitimacy of the armed forces no longer reflects a spirit of nationalism, but a political ideology with international pretensions. The military identify themselves with a political myth, for which they receive in return recognition of their task to defend and extend the political system.

(4)   The armed forces of the new nations which, though of varying political and ideological legitimation, in many cases justify their existence by their role as an integrative force and by their nation building capacity. In many new states their position is strong enough for them to seize political power and establish a regime which may or may not be openly military. Political legitimacy is impaired in such cases, however, and the armed forces are confronted with the difficult task of acting as a substitute legitimating agency.

A notable fact in practically all of these instances is that the armies concerned are mass armies, with a highly representative personnel structure. With the exception of a number of new nations, there is no serious tension between the political elite and the military establishment. The armed forces accept their subordinacy to the political culture and regard themselves as the loyal executives of the political regimes, regardless of whether the latter derive their legitimacy from traditional, legal or charismatically-determined values.

The Crisis of Legitimacy and the Militarization of Politics

The advent of the doctrine of popular sovereignty nevertheless caused considerable uncertainty regarding the legitimacy of the government. As long as the monarch had been the sole source of political authority and legitimacy, the army could only be invested with authority through him. This certainty disappeared with him.

> The dogma of *vox populi vox dei* is more amenable since there is no hard and fast definition of what is *vox* and what is *populus*. Any person and group, including the army, which succeeds in mustering a mere semblance of popular support can claim to be the lawful government. . . . Thus the path is laid wide open for the military to intervene and to supersede the civil power altogether, on the plea that they embody the sovereignty of the people.[27]

This being the case, the fact that military intervention in politics is more the exception than the rule in the developed countries might be surprising. This can be explained in two ways.

First, there is the professional concept of the military. As Huntington points out, a highly professional military elite is willing to accept full control of the civilian government.[28] For military professionalism emphasizes political neutrality and a technocratic outlook. This is so strong that even a change of regime—as in Germany in 1933 and in Czechoslovakia in 1948—meets with practically no resistance on the part of the military, despite the radical break in the legitimate political order.

Secondly, the lack of military intervention may be explained by the level of political culture. Proceeding from this concept, Finer has carried out extensive research on the role of the military in politics and has concluded that there is a close relationship between a high level of political culture and a negligible danger of military intervention. Conversely, if the level of political culture is low, the replacement of the civil authorities by military leaders may be expected.[29]

As the Western countries traditionally possess both a highly professionalized officer corps and a mature political culture, it is not surprising that despite the temptations of the doctrine of popular sovereignty military intervention in the political order is a rarity in those countries. This is evident in another way from the failure of military intervention at such dramatic moments as those occurring in Germany in 1944 and in France in 1961. Kurt Lang attributes that failure to the mature political culture of both countries and to the highly developed professional code.

> An army in whose tradition the principle of obedience to civil authority has been raised to an absolute principle cannot at the same time include an equally compelling structural imperative to engage in a *coup d'état*.[30]

The legitimate power of conviction of the regime was nevertheless highly eroded in those years, due largely to war reverses which had caused the military to lose faith in the regime. If the regime in Paris, for instance, had possessed greater authority and had united the nation behind it, the *putsch* would not have been attempted.[31] In a comparable case, the decolonization of the Dutch East Indian empire, there was nothing at all in the way of praetorianism.[32]

In the developing countries, however, where both the legitimacy and the effectiveness of civilian governments are comparatively low, military intervention will occur more frequently. Once the initial enthusiasm for independence has waned, the failure of the new civil authorities becomes increasingly apparent and finally the point is reached where the army intervenes. If they are able to guarantee law and order this does not necessarily mean that they meet the need for a legitimate government. Concentrating more on state-building than on nation-building, more on the exploitation of resources than on the mobilization of popular support,[33] they are obliged to rely upon the threat of force. They seldom succeed in resolving the crisis of legitimacy.

The Crisis of Legitimacy and the Alienation of the Military

Current civil-military relations in many Western countries are the exact opposite of the militarization of politics and society. The process now taking place is one of social penetration into the armed forces, resulting in a high degree of civilianization, isolation and alienation of the military. The crisis of legitimacy is not so much characteristic of the political order as of the military establishment.

The reason is to be found in a combination of factors. In addition to the erosion of national values and symbols and consequently of universal military service, a radical change has taken place in the values and norms of the younger generation, most of which are very much at variance with the goals and life style of the traditional military. The higher educational level of the bulk of the population and the rising level of prosperity have made military service much less attractive. Strong pacifist and anti-militarist sentiments are widening the gap between the armed forces and society still further.[34]

The armed forces are unable to screen themselves off from the changes taking place around them. The draft is an especially effective channel for outside influences. The military are on the defensive in other ways as well. For their social environment expects the armed forces to be geared as far as possible to the values and norms of civilian society, which entails civilianization, democratization, unionization and even politicization.

Developments of this kind can be viewed as actual trends, as does Moskos,[35] or as normative claims. In some parts of Western Europe, such as Scandinavia, the Netherlands and the Federal Republic of Germany, these claims are an attempt to resolve the legitimacy crisis of the armed forces and of civil-military relations by modelling the military as far as possible on civilian society. In sociological terms, this implies application of the congruence concept as it is elaborated in Eckstein's stable democracy theory.[36] He proceeds on the assumption that many different authority patterns are found in a society, while a stable democracy is possible only if there is a certain measure of congruence in authority with the pattern of government.

While Eckstein doubts the feasibility of effecting the democratization of organizations such as that of the military,[37] many radical critics in the Western countries entertain no such doubt, and state that the armed forces can only be acceptable if their internal structure and functioning coincide with those of democratic institutions. This might be viewed as being contrary to Litwak's approach, which is based not on the congruence of social institutions but on their

complementarity. Though he is concerned primarily with the complementary relations between formal organizations and primary
groups,[38] his theory seems to be equally applicable to those between
the armed forces and civilian institutions. The latter usually function
according to democratic principles in democratic countries, as is
evinced by their recognition of personal freedom and personal development, pluralism and egalitarianism. A democratic system of
this kind may be assailed from outside by the threat of force, and this
is where the specific task of the armed forces comes in. Before they
can perform their task, however, it is essential that a tremendous
concentration of arms be available and that democratic rights be
restricted. For, paradoxically enough, the armed forces operate in
a boundary area where the democratic system becomes undemocratic
for reasons of self-preservation. They operationalize and symbolize
a system of authority that becomes essential when all other possibilities are exhausted.

Regarded in this way, the alienation of the military and his
relative isolation from society are difficult to prevent.[39] The legitimation of his organization can be only partly effected by making it
consistent with the type of legitimacy of the civilian society. The
armed forces still to a certain extent have to develop their own type
of legitimacy.

THE LEGITIMATION OF VIOLENCE AND THE ARMED FORCES

Armed Forces as the Legitimate Users of Collective Violence

The problem of legitimacy is defined above as a characteristic
of the relations between the armed forces and the political community. A different approach will now be used for examining the
legitimate and illegitimate aspects of the execution of violence. This
is necessitated by the dual facts that: (1) the armed forces may be
regarded primarily as the institution that legitimately uses physical
force; and (2) many of the problems bearing upon the legitimacy of
the armed forces derive from doubts and criticism of their monopoly
of force and of military force in general.

A convenient starting point is provided by Speier, who distinguishes between two types of warfare, viz., absolute and instrumental armed conflicts.[40] The object of absolute conflicts is to effect the complete destruction of the enemy and they are characterized by an almost complete lack of restrictive measures and agreements. Such wars are waged with the consent of a large part of the political community, which also takes part in the conflict. The professional soldier is in a minority position here. Examples of this type of conflict are guerilla warfare and revolutionary war.

Instrumental armed conflicts, on the other hand, are less intensive and less brutal. They take place on the basis of elementary rules and are institutionalized to a certain extent. The object is not to destroy the enemy, but to compel him to concede defeat. The professional military and his skills are of essential importance, and he often occupies a monopoly position in the conflict.

The possibility of the military legitimation of collective violence may be expected to increase in proportion to the instrumental nature of the conflict. The unrestricted use of force will not meet with the approval of the professional military, while at the same time the legitimation of collective violence entails bearing responsibility for the weapons and methods used. The prevention of absolute conflict may in any case be expected to be prejudicial to the legitimacy claims of the professional military, who on the whole is in favor of the restriction and monopolization of violence as the only means of ensuring that full justice is done to his professionalism.

Illegitimate Violence and the Crisis of the Military

The extent and frequency of absolute conflicts have risen sharply since World War II. Though interstate wars have declined in number, domestic war has become a widespread phenomenon. Insurrectionary and revolutionary wars usually take the form of absolute conflict.

> The government aims at the elimination of the challenge to its authority; the insurrectionists aim at the capture or destruction of the government. . . . Negotiation and compromise between the contestants, which often characterize intergovernmental war, are normally lacking in domestic wars. Neither side wants to recognize the legitimacy of the other, and negotiations, much less agreements, imply such recognition.[41]

The extent to which the new types of violence may be termed legitimate or illegitimate is often a question of political choice. It is certain, however, that the definitions of legitimacy in this context are growing ever wider. Violent acts once regarded as illegitimate gradually become legitimate through a process of conscious justification.[42] The consequences for the professional military are twofold. In the first place, he loses his monopoly of the legitimate use of collective violence and is faced with competition in the form of armed civilians, resistance fighters, revolutionaries, guerilla fighters and terrorists, all of whom sooner or later claim legitimacy and even go so far as to denounce him as illegitimate. The second consequence is that the professional military feels compelled, or permits himself to be compelled, to counter this violence with similar measures. His wish to succeed leads him to use force against civilians, to torture prisoners and to deploy organized terror methods, courses of action which expose him to public criticism and to the risk of being adjudged a war criminal. Part of this process is the erosion of his own professional code, on which his self-respect and the respect of others were based.

This course of events has been perceptible in various types of conflict throughout the past fifty years. Violence of this kind was first used on a massive scale in the Japanese invasion of China and the Spanish Civil War. In World War II the German military had to contend with widespread civilian resistance, which it countered with extremely harsh measures. A third wave of absolute armed conflicts accompanied the decolonization of Asian and African regions. The countries involved included France (Southeast Asia, Algeria), the Netherlands (Indonesia) and, recently, the United States (Vietnam) and Portugal (Angola, Mozambique).

Another form of resistance is that witnessed in Hungary in 1956 and the civilian resistance of the Prague population to the Warsaw Pact troops in 1968. In the latter case the events had a demoralizing influence on the occupying forces, one of the few occasions on which this could be observed among communist troops.

Finally, there is the situation in a number of Latin American countries, where their action against urban guerilla groups and peasant insurgents has had a corrupting effect on the armed forces.

It is difficult for the military to convince the population that their hard-handed methods are justified, especially in democratic societies. The result is often that they tend to conceal their illegitimate use of violence, which they can do in colonial wars and by isolating the opponents they take prisoners. They will also try to gain new legitimacy by developing new modes of justification.[43] In some cases this may even go as far as devising a new doctrine of modern warfare answering to the demands of absolute conflict, like the idea of the *guerre révolutionnaire* worked out by the French military elite.[44]

In their endeavors to justify unpopular action the armed forces also fall back on the legal form of legitimacy by denying the legality of their opponents and emphasizing the need to maintain law and order. Referring to their opponents as "subversive elements", "terrorists", "extremists" and "bandits" is part of this general trend.[45]

The effectiveness of their measures is not without significance for the recognition of their legitimacy. If a counter-insurgency war is fought with little success the volume of criticism swells and becomes increasingly concentrated on the methods used. Accusations on the home front that the troops are committing atrocities are connected in part with those troops' inability to end the conflict.

Delegitimation of Violence and the Crisis of the Military

While the problems outlined above are largely connected with the failure of the professional formula in the confrontation with the new types of collective violence utilized by domestic and civilian resistance movements, that same traditional military professionalism is subjected to further pressure by immanent developments in military politics, strategy and technology. Two factors of decisive importance here are the deployment of nuclear weapons and the concept of strategic deterrence, both of which undermine the traditional view of the task of the military.

> Nuclear weapons weaken, but do not eliminate, the strategic concept of the inevitability of war—the essential logic of traditional military forces. . . . For the military, or at least for segments of it, mere maintenance of the technology of deterrence is a highly passive task. Either by doctrine or by training and spirit, the military requires a more active and positive outlook.[46]

Remarkably enough, it is precisely the success of the deterrence strategy—the prevention of war—which has brought about the identity crisis of the military. The more unlikely major military conflicts become, the more difficult it is for the military, not to mention his environment, to retain belief in his efforts and existence. This explains the fact that participation in dangerous and unpopular conflicts can appear attractive.

> For the army, their sense of purpose has been given a boost by the troubles in Northern Ireland. The frustrating and difficult task of preserving order in Ulster may have given little pleasure to those carrying it out, but it has reassured them, and others, of the essential requirement for their particular skills.[47]

Since activities like those of the British army in Ulster are exceptional for most military forces, however, the dilemma remains that the traditional heroic model of the military is only partly consistent with the unheroic reality of the soldier's everyday life. Nor does the role of technician or manager provide the solution, for the identity crisis is at its most severe where this role is most closely approximated.

So the question "What is military?"[48] remains a thorny one. Some seek a solution in the development of new tasks as reflected in terms like "constabulary role", "emergency tasks" and "peace-keeping operations." Others, proceeding from the partial convergence of the military and civilian occupational structures, seek it in the adoption of industrial-type organizational systems and personal policies, including unionism. The question remains, however, whether these solutions help to reinforce the legitimacy of the armed forces, for they cannot camouflage the fact that the hard core consist of nuclear weapons whose use is so unacceptable or in any event so unlikely for many people that the search for alternatives such as civil resistance systems must be termed the most positive type of effort.

If, however, the willingness to take an interest in military affairs is as slight in many Western European states as the supporters of civil resistance claim,[49] it must be considered unlikely that many people will be prepared to follow the no less difficult and risk-fraught course of civil defence. In this sense both the military and the civil defence efforts may be said to have been adversely affected by the loss of legitimacy of the national state.

NOTES

[1]David C. Rapoport, 'A Comparative Theory of Military and Political Types', in Samuel P. Huntington (ed.), *Changing Patterns of Military Politics* (N.Y.: Free Press of Glencoe, 1962), 98.

[2]Dolf Sternberger, 'Legitimacy', in David L. Sills (ed.), *International Encyclopedia of the Social Sciences* (N.Y.: Macmillan & Free Press, 1968), Vol. 9, 244 ff.

[3]Max Weber, *Grundriss der Sozialökonomik, III:* Wirtschaft und Gesellschaft (Tübingen: Mohr—Paul Siebeck, 1925, 2nd ed.), 16 ff., 122 ff.

[4]Sternberger, *op. cit.,* 244.

[5]David Easton, *A Systems Analysis of Political Life* (N.Y., 1965), 278.

[6]Seymour Martin Lipset, *Political Man: The Social Basis of Politics* (Garden City, N.Y.: Doubleday, 1960), 77.

[7]Kenneth E. Boulding, 'The Impact of the Draft on the Legitimacy of the National State', in Sol Tax (ed.), *The Draft: A Handbook of Facts and Alternatives* (Chicago and London: University of Chicago Press, 1967), 191.

[8]Niklas Luhmann, *Legitimation durch Verfahren* (Neuwied am Rhein und Berlin: Luchterhand, 1969), 28.

[9]Sandra J. Ball-Rokeach, 'The Legitimation of Violence', in James F. Short, Jr. and Marvin E. Wolfgang (eds.), *Collective Violence* (Chicago and N.Y.: Aldine—Atherton, 1972), 101; James L. Price, *Organizational Effectiveness* (Homewood, Ill.: Irwin, 1968), 49.

[10]Niklas Luhmann, *Rechtssoziologie* (Reinbek bei Hamburg: Rowolt, 1972), Vol. 2, 266.

[11]Richard Rose, 'Dynamic Tendencies in the Authority of Regimes', *World Politics,* Vol. XXI (July 1969), 606.

[12]William A. Gamson, Power and Discontent (1968), quotation in Ted Robert Gurr, *Why Men Rebel* (Princeton, N.J.: Princeton U.P., 1970), 185.

[13]Talcott Parsons, *Structure and Process in Modern Societies* (Ill.: Free Press of Glencoe, 1960), 20 f., 60-65; James D. Thompson, *Organizations in Action* (N.Y.: McGraw-Hill, 1967), 10 ff.; Price, *op. cit.,* 49 ff.

[14]J. P. Nettl, *Political Mobilization* (London: Faber and Faber, 1967), 198.

[15]Luhmann, *Legitimation . . . , op. cit.,* 27 ff.; Luhmann, Rechtssoziologie, *op. cit.,* 259 ff.

[16]Amitai Etzioni, *The Active Society* (London—N.Y.: Collier-Macmillan and Free Press, 1968), 360 f.

[17]Easton, *op. cit.,* 267 ff., 273 f.

[18]George Caspar Homans, *Social Behavior: Its Elementary Forms* (N.Y.: Harcourt, Brace & World, 1961), 386.

[19]Luhmann, *Rechtssoziologie, op. cit.,* 67 f.; see also the theory on institutionalization from Arnold Gehlen, *Anthropologische Forschung* (Reinbek bei Hamburg: Rowoht, 1961), 70 ff.

[20]Luhmann, *Rechtssoziologie, op. cit.,* 260 ff.

[21]Karl W. Deutsch, *The Nerves of Government* (N.Y.: Free Press; London: Collier-Macmillan, 1966, 2nd ed.), 153.

[22]Lipset, *op. cit.,* 77.

[23]For critical reflections see Brian M. Barry, *Sociologists, Economists and Democracy* (London: Collier-Macmillan, 1970), 63 ff.; also Price, *op. cit.*, 49 ff.

[24]David E. Apter, *The Politics of Modernization* (Chicago and London: The University of Chicago Press, 1967), 236 f.

[25]An attempt to work along these lines: Jacques van Doorn and Jan H. Mans, 'United Nations Forces: On Legitimacy and Effectiveness of International Military Operations', in Jacques van Doorn (ed.), *Armed Forces and Society: Sociological Essays* (The Hague—Paris: Mouton, 1968), 347 ff.

[26]Samuel P. Huntington, *Political Order in Changing Society* (New Haven and London: Yale U.P., 1969), 1.

[27]S. E. Finer, *The Man on Horseback: The Role of the Military in Politics* (London and Dunmow: Pall Mall, 1962), 208.

[28]Samuel P. Huntington, *The Soldier and the State* (Cambridge, Mass.: Harvard U.P., 1959), 83 ff.

[29]Finer, *op. cit.*, 86 ff.; Huntington, *Political Order . . .*, *op. cit.*, 194.

[30]Kurt Lang, 'The Military Putsch in a Developed Political Culture: Confrontations of Military and Civilian Power in Germany and France', in Jacques van Doorn (ed.), *Armed Forces and Society: Sociological Essays* (The Hague—Paris: Mouton, 1968), 217.

[31]John Steward Ambler, *Soldiers against the State: The French Army in Politics* (Garden City, N.Y.: Doubleday, 1968), 398 ff.

[32]R. Kroes, 'Decolonialization and the Military: The Case of the Netherlands. A Study on Political Reaction', in Morris Janowitz and Jacques van Doorn (eds.), *On Military Intervention* (Rotterdam: University Press, 1971), 95 ff.

[33]C. J. Welch, Jr. (ed.), *Soldier and State in Africa* (Evanston, 1970), 48.

[34]The American situation: Morris Janowitz, *The U.S. Forces and the Zero Draft* (London: I.I.S.S., 1973), 4 f.

[35]Charles Moskos, Jr., 'The Emergent Military: Civil, Traditional, or Plural?', *Pacific Sociological Review*, Vol. XVI (April 1973), 256 f., 267 ff.

[36]Harry Eckstein, *Division and Cohesion in Democracy: A Study of Norway* (N.J.: Princeton U.P., 1966), 225-87.

[37]Eckstein, *op. cit.*, 237 f.

[38]E. Litwak, 'Extended Kin Relations in an Industrial Democratic Society', in E. Shanas and F. G. Streib (eds.), *Social Structure and the Family: Generational Relations* (New Jersey: Prentice-Hall, 1965), 313 f.; E. Litwak and H. J. Meyer, 'A Balance Theory of Coordination between Bureaucratic Organizations and Community Primary Groups', *Administrative Science Quarterly, Vol. XI* (June 1966), 31 ff.

[39]Laurence I. Radway, 'Recent Trends at American Service Academies', in Charles C. Moskos, Jr. (ed.), *Public Opinion and the Military Establishment* (Beverly Hills, Cal.: SAGE Publications, 1971), 9: 'in a nation where Spartan attributes are in short supply, any institution which feels a need for them must seek some protection by isolating itself from civilian society'.

[40]H. Speier, 'The Social Types of War', *The American Journal of Sociology*, Vol. 46 (1940-41), 445-54. The typology is applied by Ger Teitler, *Toepassing van geweld* (Meppel: Boom, 1972), 14-34.

[41]Samuel P. Huntington, 'Patterns of Violence in World Politics', in Samuel P. Huntington (ed.), *Changing Patterns of Military Politics* (N.Y.: Free Press of Glencoe, 1962), 21.

[42]Ball-Rokeach, *op. cit.,* 105 f.

[43]Ball-Rokeach, *op. cit.,* 106 f.; Ambler, *op. cit.,* 183; Jacques van Doorn, 'Justifying Military Action: The Dutch Return to Indonesia 1945-1949', in Morris Janowitz and Jacques van Doorn (eds.), *On Military Ideology* (Rotterdam: University Press, 1971), 77 ff.

[44]Peter Paret, *French Revolutionary Warfare from IndoChina to Algeria: The Analysis of a Political and Military Doctrine* (N.Y.: Praeger, 1964).

[45]Van Doorn, 'Justifying Military Action . . .', *op. cit.,* 81 f.

[46]Janowitz, 'The U.S. Forces and the Zero Draft', *op. cit.,* 3.

[47]J. C. M. Baynes, *The Soldier in Modern Society* (London: Eyre Methuen, 1972), 92.

[48]Albert D. Biderman, 'What is Military', in Sol Tax (ed.), *The Draft* (Chicago and London: The University of Chicago Press, 1967), 122 ff.

[49]Adam Roberts, 'Alternatives to Existing Forces', *Force in Modern Societies: The Military Profession* (London: I.I.S.S., 1973), 27.

Part Three

EXECUTION AND
CONTROL OF FORCE

JUSTIFYING MILITARY ACTION:
THE DUTCH RETURN TO INDONESIA 1945-49

"MISSION INTERRUPTED"

*T*he end of World War II in Europe in May 1945 completed the liberation of the Netherlands but left the Dutch East Indies still under Japanese occupation. At that moment thousands of Dutch troops from the southern provinces of the country were already in training and their numbers soon swelled to more than two infantry divisions. Though impoverished and exhausted by five years of German occupation, the Dutch lost no time in building an expeditionary force to join the Allies in the Pacific.

But they came too late. At the time of the sudden surrender of Japan (15 August, 1945) only very weak Dutch forces were operating in the Far East. They were totally incapable of taking over the Indies from the Japanese military administration, which they had to leave in control until some months later, when British and Indian troops were ready to move into the main cities of Java and Sumatra.

Those few months, however, had been sufficient for a group of Indonesian leaders to proclaim an independent Republic of Indonesia and to gain some popular support, especially from the people of Java. Attempts by the British troops to assume control in the main cities, and the return of the Dutch from the Japanese internment camps soon led to irregular fighting, which gave rise to bitter resistance by armed young Indonesians. A disastrous wave of anti-Dutch and Anti-European feeling swept over the main islands, claiming thousands of victims among the Dutch and Chinese minorities. In

111

some places, notably at Surabaya, British and Indian troops killed thousands of young Indonesian guerilla fighters, thus broadening the gap between the young Republic and the British and Dutch interim administration.

When the British left in the autumn of 1946 a state of intermittent warfare and political bargaining continued for several years, until finally the Republic of Indonesia was recognized by the Dutch. The Dutch troops, by then increased to 150,000, tried to overrun the Republic in two campaigns, both of which were terminated by order of the Security Council and were followed by long periods of insurgency warfare throughout the whole of Java and in parts of the Outer Islands. At last, forced by international pressure and by its obvious inability to end the Indonesian guerilla, the Netherlands decided to transfer sovereignty to Indonesia (December 1949).[1]

The story of the conflict is a story of collective frustration. During the four years of Japanese occupation, the Dutch East Indies had undergone a fundamental change. The Dutch part of the population—about 250,000 people, 70% of them born in the Indies—returned in 1945 from the camps to a society in full political and social mobilization. Having only just survived the Japanese terror, they now had to face the fanatical attacks of a youth which was trained and indoctrinated by their hated foe and headed by radical nationalists who had been in Dutch internment before the war.

To their sense of alienation in their own country was added a feeling of bitterness about the critical attitude adopted by the Allies they had voluntarily joined in 1941 when Japan launched its offensive in the Pacific, The Dutch in the Indies felt 'the winds of change', now referred to as the era of decolonization, earlier than the French and the Belgians in their colonies.

Criticism was not confined to the international world; part of the national scene was critical too. During all the years of the conflict the home front was divided, with political parties overtly voicing the wish to give up the South East Asian part of the empire. The Dutch in the colony felt ever more strongly that they were aboard a sinking ship.

Although the Indonesian Republic was acknowledged *de jure* at the end of 1949, the feeling of disappointment and humiliation did not vanish at once. The Dutch were to function as a scapegoat for a further 15 years. Even now, more than a quarter of a century later, there is a traumatic consciousness among a great number of the Hollanders who were connected in some way with the Indonesian drama.

Such a case of collective frustration must surely represent a case of collective justification, as in fact it does. The whole complex of conditions is there, varying from emotional bonds, social commitments, legal rights and economic interests, and providing in combination a most solid base on which to erect a monument of ideological definitions of the conflict.

In the following pages we shall discuss briefly the various patterns of ideology developed in the five years of the struggle, the empirical background of these evaluations, and the sources of the stubborn search for self-justification continued despite the widening credibility gap. The emphasis will be on the role of the military.

PATTERNS OF IDEOLOGY

Ideological justifications are often drawn from the situation at hand. Those concerned are trying to defend themselves by referring to the unbearable conditions which they feel will make their method of handling the problem more readily understood.

In major questions, however, past experience will be mobilized as well. If the problem has been a subject of discussion for a long time, it is not difficult to deploy old arguments in the search for adapted justification.

Both sorts of arguments were used in the Indonesian conflict. The dubious origins of the young Indonesian Republic and its inability to control the situation provided the Dutch with sufficient reason to intervene. The most important arguments, however, had long served traditional political claims. As a colonial elite, the Dutch policy-makers had defended their role and position against the rising tide of Asian nationalism. Now that stormy weather was ahead, they repeated all the old traditional arguments in a last effort to influence a disapproving international opinion.

The impossible nation. One of the strongest objections against the rise of the Republic of Indonesia was the denial that "Indonesia" in fact existed at all, either ethnically or politically. It was claimed that it consisted of no more than an incohesive collection of peoples without common culture or race and without any political identity. The general standpoint of Dutch colonial policy had been voiced many times in the past century, including by the statesman and colonial expert Colijn in 1928:

> The term Indonesia which is often used to express a national unity is without meaning. The isles of the East Indies archipelago are a unity for the simple reason that they constitute the *Dutch* East Indies, and for that reason only.[2]

So the name "Indonesia" retained a revolutionary meaning, a sort of provocation used by radicals which was obviously intended to symbolize an independent and future unity against the colonial power.

In proclaiming the Republic of Indonesia in 1945 the nationalist leaders in fact proclaimed the rise of this non-existent political unity. The entire machinery of Dutch conservatism could be expected to oppose this claim:

> There are at least seven nationalities on Java and Sumatra alone. . . . This state is quite certainly predestined to disintegrate after a time.[3]

> In speaking of the granting of independence to Indonesia one should not forget that it comprises 66 peoples totalling in all some 70 millions who inhabit an archipelago as vast as Europe. . . .

> Reference to Indonesia and Indonesians in any news bulletin can only be be considered to be a means of propaganda intended to suggest that 66 peoples are one people, one nation, which of course presents a completely false picture.[4]

The flow of information to the Dutch troops was based on the same theme:

> The Dutch East Indies with its numerous completely different races is not a geographical area of homogeneous people called "Indonesians" as the anti-propaganda forces would like to have us believe. The many peoples of the archipelago are so distinctive that any attempt to force them into a unity with the collective noun "Indonesians" is as foolish as the assertion that all Europeans are one people.[5]

This was not an academic debate but the basis of the federal system, developed before the war and continued in the post-war period by the successive establishment of a number of Dutch-backed states in the Outer Islands.[6] The overt and consistently pursued goal was the reduction of the Republic of Indonesia to a "Republic of Djocja", as it came to be called.

The contaminated Republic. A charge leveled with even greater frequency against the Republic was that it was a Japanese creation, the product of manipulation on the part of the Japanese regime.

A Dutch parliamentary delegation concluded after a visit to Indonesia in March and April 1946:

> Thus the "Repoeblik Indonesia" was born, made in Japan, under Japanese supervision and under two leaders who during the years of oppression had served the Japanese war effort and supported by a power which was instructed and educated by the Japanese and was penetrated throughout by Japanese ideas.[7]

This argument was heard repeatedly in the following years. Its tremendous popular impact is hardly surprising, for in the post-war period there was no more damning accusation than that of collaboration with the enemy. The Indonesian objection to Dutch policy, namely that the federal states were "made by the Dutch", was readily countered with the argument that the Indonesian Republic was "made in Japan".[8]

For the Dutch troops this propaganda had a very special significance. The first divisions were formed in the closing stages of World War II for the purpose of joining the Allies in the war against Japan. In addition, some of the troops were recruited directly among members of the resistance movement against the German occupation, which meant that they were extremely sensitive on the point of political collaboration.

Moreover, the argument was effective because the change in the war aims, i.e., the substitution of the Republican nationalists for the Japanese, was made easier in that the former could be labeled as accomplices. The military operations were justified as being a purge of the Indonesian regime from traitors and war criminals. This interpretation was bound to find fervent support among the members of the Dutch colonial forces (KNIL), who had suffered a great deal at Japanese hands and who thus had many reasons for wishing to erase all Japanese influence.

Furthermore, the troop commanders were ordered to devote special attention to Japanese deserters who had joined the Indonesian army and who were sometimes taken prisoner. They were assumed to be the hard core of Republican resistance, though in actual fact there was only a small number of Japanese deserters in the Indonesian army.[9]

The idea of a Japanese-contaminated Republic seems to have been of durable ideological value. As late as October 1949, during the Round Table Conference which preceded the transfer of sovereignty two months later, Dutch-oriented Irian leaders pleaded in favor of an autonomous Irian Barat (West New Guinea) because, as they argued, the Indonesian Republic displayed "Japanese tendencies."[10]

Yet another infection seemed gradually to gain in value as an argument against the Indonesian cause: the penetration of communism. Communist Indonesian leaders and organizations had been actively involved in the struggle for independence from the time of its inception. On the internal front they made repeated attempts to overrule the nationalist government in Djocja.[11] These facts were eagerly exploited by Dutch propaganda, which suggested that independence for Indonesia could result in a communist regime.

A typical example of this approach was a pamphlet entitled *"Naar de Sovjet Republiek Indonesia"* (Toward the Soviet Republic of Indonesia) written by a prominent opponent of the official Dutch policy and published by the Information Service of a very influential pressure group, the so-called National Committee for the Maintenance of a Unified Empire.[12] The general tenor of this pamphlet was that Indonesian nationalism was no more than a smoke screen for international communism, and was supported by the Soviet Union. It suggested that the past political careers of all prominent nationalist leaders—Sukarno, Hatta, Sjahrir—were dubious ones in that they had had relations with communist organizations.

This argument did not penetrate to the lower army echelons, but was acclaimed only at top level, especially among intelligence officers of the political branch.

Legitimacy and legality. The political debate about the Indonesian problem was to a large extent dominated by legal arguments. The main attack on the progressive Dutch politicians and parties was largely based on the argument that the constitution was at stake.[13] Throughout the whole of the conflict the Republic of Indonesia was assumed to have no rights whatsoever, and it was accorded only a hesitant *de facto* recognition.

This being the case, the Dutch army was free to label its military opponent "subversive elements", "extremists" and "terrorists", operating in bands wrongly claiming to constitute a regular armed force. There could be only one army in Indonesia: the one serving the Dutch government.

This legalistic background explains the name given to the first and second military campaign against the Indonesian Republic (medio 1947 and end 1948), which were organized as large-scale military operations with tanks, artillery and bombers, but were nevertheless labeled *"politionele acties"* (police actions). It was formally admitted that this was the usual term applied to all activity of the Dutch colonial army connected with internal conflicts.[14]

The attitude of the Dutch government made it possible for the troops to define the Indonesian armed resistance in terms either of insurrection or of crime. Often there was no distinction made between Indonesian regular forces, guerilla units and bandits. This accounts for court-martialling and execution of regular Indonesian soldiers and officers taken prisoner in Dutch-controlled territory.[15] Although legally admissible, these and other sentences symbolized the fundamental difference in the legal position of the protagonists' forces. For after all, the Indonesian army was supposed to be an insurgency force, not a military opponent.

Law and order. Formally and informally the most frequently used and most popular argument employed by the Dutch was that it was by no means the intention for the Dutch forces to occupy the country; they were simply there to suppress the terrorists in order to protect the population. The tens of thousands of patrol orders all contained the same stereotyped wording: "Destroy the enemy forces; arrest suspects; gain the confidence of the population."

In the Dutch military ideology the only major distinction seemed to be the line drawn between the Indonesian population—victims of terror—and the enemy, i.e., the terrorists, who were first and foremost the enemies of their own people. The military mission was officially conducted in terms of "Justice and Security" or "Law and Order."

All troops were indoctrinated with this pattern of justification, particularly those brought in from Holland. It often started with a letter from the commanding officer to the parents of the enlisted man, saying:

> The Japanese occupation has caused a crisis which the population of the Netherlands Indies cannot resolve without the help of others. The Netherlands, which has been in contact with the inhabitants for more than 300 years, is the obvious country to provide such help. Our army has now been entrusted with the task of restoring law and order to the East Indies, which is incapable of performing this action alone.[16]

On disembarkation in Indonesia the soldiers themselves received a letter from the Commander-in-Chief himself:

> The Japanese occupation and its consequences—lawlessness, terror, poverty, hunger—destroyed the foundations and disintegrated the social order. This situation did not end with the Japanese surrender. Too many irresponsible elements—unfortunately part of every nation—took advantage of the disorder and the lasting defencelessness of their own people.[17]

The second military action against the Republic of Indonesia was motivated in the same way. In the words of the Order of the Day issued by the Commander-in-Chief on 17 December 1948:

> Remember that you are bearers of justice and security to a population that has long been subjected to terror and oppression.[18]

The final cease-fire in August 1949 necessitated cooperation between the Dutch and Indonesian forces. The Commander-in-Chief now had to give another interpretation of the army's maintenance of law and order:

> We were termed "the strange army" . . . . We came as a fighting force but nevertheless as a friend which was compelled to act as an enemy in a country whose population was seen as friends to be protected. Now we shall no longer fight against the Republican Army, but with it, since the Indonesian army shares with us a duty to protect the population against the marauding bands.[19]

For the military, and particularly for the KNIL, this part of the ideology was of major importance. Formally, as armed police supporting the ordinary police forces in the colony, their first task was to take action against the rebels. As long as it was possible to define the situation as a temporary state of disturbance there was no need to worry about a justification of armed action, which could be regarded simply as part of a police-and-judicial control pattern, and not a real military action.

It may be concluded that it is possible to differentiate between the social, political, legal and police arguments, all of which avoided any suggestion that the Dutch military were fighting a war. They were simply restoring the social and political order which in their view had proved to be the most appropriate system for the population of Indonesia. The Indonesian Republic lacked not only the legal basis needed to provide an acceptable alternative, but was moreover incapable of protecting its people from the consequences of the social disintegration following Japanese occupation. So the Republic was declared a failure on the double score of legitimacy and effectiveness.

This interpretation was formulated at the highest levels of Dutch policy, officially voiced and unofficially supported by an impressive number of colonial experts. The military establishment absorbed and accepted this evaluation and was provided with arguments from above. It played no substantial or autonomous part in the development of the pattern of justification; it simply made use of it.

HARD FACTS AND SELECTIVE PERCEPTION

Ideologies always contain an element of truth. They derive their special significance from their interwoven threads of empirical observations and distorted perception. So ideologies can be distinguished from outright lies and propaganda on the one hand, and from a serious intellectual approach to reality on the other.

For the ideological patterns discussed above the same sort of distinction has to be made between factual observation and selective perception. The centuries-long interaction between the Dutch rulers and the Indonesian population and the thorough study of Indonesia by Dutch specialists guaranteed sufficient knowledge of the real situation in the colony, even taking into account the fact that the sudden political and psychological breakthrough which started in 1942 had changed the scene entirely.

On the other hand it was precisely this close contact, always from a position of absolute power and authority, that made it difficult for the Dutch to make judgements without being influenced by distortive emotions and shortsighted perception. Foreigners often tended to come closer to the truth than the Dutch insiders who stuck to their policy until its credibility was entirely exhausted.

Before proceeding to an attempt to explain this obstinate determination to justify the Dutch position, we shall deal briefly with the extent to which these ideologies found a more or less solid basis in the reality of post-war Indonesia.

The viability of the Indonesian Republic. The post-war federal policy developed by the Dutch had a history of at least fifty years. It might even be stated that the Dutch traditionally preferred decentralized administration to centralized control. The enormous distances were not the only factor here; of greater importance was the fundamental idea that the ethnic, religious and cultural heterogeneity of the population was far too great to allow of a uniform policy.

The system of indirect rule adopted had much to do with this standpoint, not only for the tactical political profit it promised but also as a means of keeping intact the plurality of Indonesian culture and society.

Both conventional wisdom and ethnographic knowledge contributed to the insight that it would be almost impossible to press the given heterogeneity into a common pattern. The Dutch had ample reason to assume that the idea of a unified Indonesian Republic would prove to be either a false claim of a small group of Java-centered leaders or an illusion that was symptomatic of the naivety of the revolutionary situation.

Now, twenty years later, it has to be acknowledged that Dutch pessimism has found support from recent political events and from newer studies of Indonesian culture. The unitary state was scarcely in existence (1950) when tensions arose between the Javanese center and what the Dutch had termed "the Outer Territories" (Buitengewesten), culminating in the late fifties in a civil war which continued for three years.

Specialists in Indonesian history and culture have since recognized the dichotomy between Java and Outer Indonesia which, though masked by colonial rule, is rooted in an older cultural matrix.[20]

Yet the arguments put forward at the time by the Dutch must be labeled as ideological in that they entirely underestimated the impact of post-war nationalism as a unifying force and particularly as a force directed against Dutch intervention. What was ideological in the narrower sense was the hesitation to promote unification because the major argument employed stressed historical heterogeneity and not future politics, thus giving direct support to the interests of Dutch policy in the East.

The charge that the Republic of Indonesia was a Japanese creation was much weaker. It was quite true that the nationalist leaders had accepted Japanese help and owed their success in the initial stages of insurrection to Japanese manipulation. It was also true that the Republic, imitating the Japanese in many visible cultural aspects like the training, uniform and ritual of the armed forces, could not but arouse deeply-felt abhorrence among the Dutch ex-repatriates and ex-prisoners.

But the constant use of these points as a political argument against the rise of Indonesian nationalism was evidently insufficient. The Japanese were extremely unpopular, as evidenced by an armed Indonesian insurrection in the last year of occupation. The first attacks of the nationalist *Pemudas* (revolutionary youth) were primarily directed against the Japanese military.[21] Moreover, the argument lost its substance at the end of World War II, when Japan was eliminated as a political factor. It was not only untrue, but ineffective as well.

The suggestion of a communist infection of the Indonesian Republic had much more relevance and effectiveness, particularly in the years of the Cold War and the rise of Communist China. The *coup* engineered by Muso and other communist leaders in Madiun (September 1948) and supported by about 25,000 troops demonstrated once again the real danger of a communist regime in this part of the world.[22] It was speedily followed, however, by a demonstration of force by the central government, which soon succeeded in putting down the rebellion.

This event strengthened the international position of the Republic, particularly in the view of the United States, eager to support any regime that proved capable of controlling its communists at home. The Muso rebellion was a test-case whereby the Dutch argument lost its value in the eyes of the American government. Soon afterwards when it embarked upon the second military action (December 1948), the Dutch were to find that American support had changed sides.

Terrorist tactics against the civilian population. The rise of the Indonesian Republic followed a period of serious social disruption caused by the Japanese occupation. Millions were impoverished, largely owing to the closure of the big agricultural estate, hundreds of thousands experienced forced labor or served in the Japanese army as auxiliary soldiers.

In the last months of 1945, when Japanese authority had disappeared but not been replaced by either Allied or Dutch forces, revolutionary uprisings were accompanied by waves of mass criminality. After that terrifying time of suffering and humiliation the majority of the Dutch population there tended to identify the Indonesian cause with chaos and terror.

There is sufficient empirical evidence that in the years of the Dutch-Indonesian conflict the Republican forces did not succeed in controlling the considerable numbers of criminal bands in the countryside. In addition, guerilla groups often employed force and even terror to obtain food and money from the population.

It is also quite true that the Dutch troops were often more effective in guaranteeing law and order. By providing massive material and technical aid and expertise, the Dutch military take-over of former Republican regions marked the start of economic progress for the population.

These facts made it fairly simple for the Dutch to obscure the difference between the Republican forces and the criminal elements. Because this difference was vague and gradual, it was easy to suggest that the Indonesian army could hardly be regarded as a respectable regular army and that it bore full responsibility for the hardships of the population.

The Dutch interpretation of affairs gave full emphasis to the

fact—common in every revolutionary war—that the struggle between the opponents was for the loyalty of the population, so that
in a sense the war was conducted like an agonizing and bloody elec-
tion campaign.[23] In struggles of this kind terrorism is the weapon of
the weak. Unable to withstand the attacks of the Dutch army in the
open field, the Indonesian resistance concentrated on hit and run
operations and on pressing the civilians to hide and supply the
guerilla fighters.

The accusation of terrorism might be justified in a large number
of cases, but the reverse side of the medal was the Dutch use of
counter-terror tactics, as in the southern Celebes (Sulawesi) where
the notorious Special Forces of Captain Raymond Westerling killed
at least several thousands of civilians to gain control of the chaotic
situation.[24]

Even though actions of this kind were exceptional, the Dutch
tolerated a general policy of intimidating the Indonesian population
by mass arrests and the use of torture on suspect prisoners. It would
be hypocritical to ignore this aspect of the struggle, as is usually the
case in Dutch commentaries.[25]

The silence systematically observed on this "terror-torture
cycle"[26] is perhaps the most significant aspect of the Dutch justification of the military intervention. By comparing the pacification
efforts of the Dutch army with the terrorist practices of scattered
bands of Indonesian guerilla fighters Dutch military authorities built
up a real ideological picture. It is a picture requiring completion by
reference to the official *Tentara Republik Indonesia* as a considerable pacifying force and to the widespread Dutch police brutality.

A last question still remains to be answered: how are we
to account for the fact that for some four years the Dutch stuck to
their largely false interpretation of the situation and to their distorted perception of the conflict and its gradual escalation? The
question is especially important in view of the fact that the Dutch
government succeeded in retaining the support of the majority of the
Dutch population throughout the full period of the conflict. Public
opinion polls showed that the hawkish approach to the problem
never failed to find widespread support among the voters.[27] How are
we to explain the absence of a credibility gap?

SOURCES OF IDEOLOGY

Conditions for ideological distortion can be divided into two categories. The first concerns the factors which directly influence the perceptive process, like the amount of information provided and the degree of emotional commitment; the second category includes the indirect causes, such as the social basis of intellectual distortion (vested interests etc.). A lesser-known third element, the self-propelling aspect of ideological justification, will be discussed separately in a later section.

Collective humiliation. It is clear from several elaborate studies that the revolt of the French army had definitely been provoked by long years of humiliation.[28] Though the Dutch KNIL suffered from similar frustration it never defied the Dutch government. A recent analysis by Kroes has made it amply clear that praetorianism played only a marginal role.[29]

Yet the Dutch East Indies army had many good reasons to feel angry and even desperate. In 1942 it had been defeated by the Japanese in a way that could hardly be considered to be honorable. After only a few weeks the strong Dutch forces on Java and Sumatra had surrendered, in many places with little resistance. In addition, their defeat was plainly visible to the native population, traditionally prepared to accept the superiority of the Dutch and now suddenly confronted with a total breakdown of the rulers' apparatus under a single blow from a poorly equipped Asian force.

In the prisoner of war and internment camps humiliation was experienced even more deeply. A policy of continued submittance supported by harsh methods of punishment deepened the hatred of the Dutch military and civilian population for the Japanese. The internees, separated from their wives and children, waited four years for the moment when they would have the chance to avenge themselves.

The end of the war, however, did not end humiliation. Far from resuming their former position of power, they had to endure the street terror of young Indonesians and the rising tide of revolution. While the Japanese authorities and the new Indonesian leaders and their supporters struggled for control in the country, the Dutch military, unarmed and utterly exhausted, were ordered to stay in the camps.

When finally, many months later, they had gathered sufficient power to take the initiative a long and laborious bargaining process started between the Dutch government and the Indonesian leaders. Time and again the Dutch troops clashed with the less disciplined Republican army staffed partly by ex-KNIL soldiers who could only be regarded as traitors. The first military action, in the summer of 1947, was stopped by order of the Security Council, and bargaining started again. The forced cease-fire was supervised by United Nations Military Observers, which was experienced as a national insult.

This story of continued humiliation at both the personal and institutional levels contains the first explanation of ideological defence. Unable to accept the new situation and prevented from restoring the old order of things, the military were very much inclined to seek unrealistic explanations. The frustration and disgust were focused on the scapegoats at hand: the Japanese, their Indonesian collaborators, the Allies not prepared to take a hard line, the Dutch politicians—some of them without colonial experience and therefore considered to be utterly naive—and, behind these personal failures, the invisible hand of British colonial interests and world communism. As far as emotional factors can provide an explanation of the distortion of social perception, all conditions were fulfilled.

Limited information. The perception of events was also distorted by a lack of information about what had happened during the Japanese occupation of the Indies. Even for a detached observer without emotional ties with the country the uprising of the Indonesians in the critical post-war months came as a complete surprise. The information possessed by the Allied and Dutch intelligence services had been scant in the extreme. They had been sufficiently informed about the activities of the Japanese and their efforts to mobilize the population against the Allied forces, but little was known about the success of this policy.

During the war the Dutch inside the colony were completely

isolated in internment camps and were not permitted to have any contact with the Indonesian population. Little was known of the new nationalist organizations and their political claims, which were not considered to be a serious threat. Even left-wing camp groups proved to be conservative in their plans and proposals on their return to freedom and post-war Indonesian reality.

Separation of the Dutch- and Indonesian-controlled territories was effected in the second half of 1945. In the following years only small groups of Dutch politicians and journalists visited the Indonesian Republic. The Dutch were again isolated from the course of events in the nationalist camp, which meant that once again they lacked first-hand information.

This self-chosen isolation was reinforced by the governmental and military manipulation of what little information there was. The propaganda machinery of the Dutch was mobilized to minimize the achievements of the young Republic and to emphasize its failures, which were indeed considerable and frequent. Conservative groups in Holland obtained their information about the course of the conflict sometimes directly from the political intelligence services.[30]

The Dutch forces not only manipulated information but also suffered from its incapacity to interpret the nature of the developing guerilla war and the immanent danger of its escalation into a scarcely controllable armed conflict. Right from the beginning the KNIL generals underestimated the strength of the Republican resistance.[31] Their miscalculation now causes no surprise in the light of the later experiences of the French in Algeria and the Americans in Vietnam, neither of which managed a more realistic evaluation of their situation.

All in all, the limited amount of knowledge and the little-understood failure of the Dutch politicians and military forces to gain control of the situation gave rise to a flow of justifications. Up to the end of the conflict stress was constantly placed on the distinction between the "small group of irresponsible elements" which had seized control with the aid of force and even terror, and the mass of the population, eager to accept Dutch rule. The Netherlands only had to stand firm both politically and militarily, for it was in a position to offer an acceptable alternative to what was assumed to be a *va banc* policy of the regime in Djocja. It was not until the last year that, after having failed to overrun the heartland of the Republic, the Dutch were reluctantly prepared to acknowledge their various miscalculations. Bitter experience proved to be the only way of revealing the irrelevance of the false interpretations of the "Indonesian question."

Vested interests. Part of this miscalculation was inevitable. The Dutch were the first nation to experience the post-war decolonization process, and to be forced to decide how to cope with a major revolt inside their colonial empire. In 1945 and 1946, the crucial years in Dutch policy formulation, it was not easy to foresee that only fifteen years later even the African continent would have been decolonized.

Looking back, it is extremely difficult to reconstruct the collective outlook of the first post-war generation. Confronted with a highly incomprehensive and complex situation, they tended to rely on the judgement of insiders and experts. Because of the unexpected development of events, however, the solutions suggested by the specialists could only refer to earlier experience. As a consequence, many interpretations of the Indonesian conflict referred to historical situations rather than future developments.

The pattern of ideology presented by the Dutch may thus be classified as typically conservative, in fact as a plea for the *status quo.* The ideas put forward were supported by a general feeling of nostalgia, particularly among the Eurasian population which longed for *tempo doeloe* (old times).

Reference to vested interests as a major source of collective justification should therefore not be restricted to the field of economic advantages, but must be understood as covering the whole field of human experience. In colonial conflicts in particular, when part of the 'establishment' has an emotional investment in the existing order, the strong tensions generated express themselves in anxiety and distorted ideas.

Various sorts of vested interests were accumulated in the Dutch East Indies. The major cause of ideological distortion was the existential bond of at least half the Dutch minority with the country. These emotional investments also had social and institutional roots since nearly all key positions in the colony were in the hands of the Dutch. One might even say that the institutional superstructure—

government administration, army, schools, plantations and churches
—was above all part of the Dutch acculturation process and was consequently experienced as a Dutch achievement. This included the
purely economic interests forming part of the existing order: the
majority of the Dutch population felt that they were sure to be ex-
pelled sooner or later after independence.

This expectation or at least the general feeling of uncertainty
about the future resulted in over-emphasis of the Dutch contribution
to the colony. The traditional feeling of ethnic and national superiority developed into an overt ideology which manifested itself in strong
paternalistic attitudes, the restoration of former Dutch positions
and a general tenor of opinion that the future Indonesian state should
in any case be integrated in a Dutch-controlled commonwealth.

The Dutch military establishment in the Indies was one of the
main pillars of the colonial upper class. Kroes has shown that 40% of
the senior officers of the KNIL were born in the colony and have to
be classified as a group that had staked everything on a career in the
Indies.[32] The lower ranks, the non-commissioned officers and the
rank and file, were largely Eurasians and members of what was called
in the British colonies "the martial races" of the archipelago
(Amboinese, Menadonese, and others), many of them Christian, and
all of them ardently devoted to the Dutch cause.

So the hard core of the Dutch troops in Indonesia had ample
reason to fear any change in the colonial *status quo*. Their social and
professional existence depended on the continuity of the colonial
situation. Among the military the idea of Western superiority and
its concomitant contempt for the Indonesians took the form of a
feeling of military superiority. Their corporate ideology, supported
by their membership of certain ethnic minorities, resulted in a serious
miscalculation regarding the rapid surrender of the Indonesian
rebels.

In fact most Dutch military never felt serious doubts about the
outcome of the armed conflict. They claimed superiority and, in a
way, they were superior. Though it is true that they failed to cope
with the guerilla of the Republic, it is also true that the Indonesian
forces never succeeded in gaining a victory, even a minor one, against
Dutch troops. Viewed against this background it is clear that the
military failed to adapt their ideas to the political reality of the

moment, maintaining up to the last stage of the conflict that the Indonesians could easily be defeated by force, which was the only adequate answer in the circumstances.

"Point of no return." Because a conflict is a process, the ideological interpretation of conflicts can only be adequately understood as a result of the process. A "latent ideology"[33] is probably always in existence, but it only becomes manifest, and grows into a motivational force, in the course of action.

In virtually every preface to the records of Dutch divisions, brigades and regiments stationed in the Indies, a highly characteristic statement expressing the feeling of the troops is found: *"de offers kúnnen niet vergeefs zijn geweest"* (the sacrifices cannot have been in vain).

This feeling can be generalized. The Dutch population had suffered long years of hardship during and after the period of Japanese occupation. Many of them had lost relatives and all of them returned from the camps destitute, and exhausted by illness and hunger. Yet many of them felt obliged to pick up the threads of the pre-war years and did their utmost to restore the disorganized public services and the destroyed plantations, bringing in new machinery and vehicles that had been bought by groups of Dutch specialists in Australian exile.[34]

The technical, economic and organizational reconstruction continued for several years despite serious difficulties and setbacks. Stimulated by the enormous demand for raw materials a policy of expanding investments was pursued in the expectation of short-term profits from the world market prices and a long-term restoration of the previous situation.

Politically the commitments were even stronger. The federal policy of the Dutch government led to the emergence of a number of Dutch-sponsored states which offered a wide variety of political and administrative positions to Indonesians. Many Indonesian aristocratic rulers, in particular, succumbed to the temptation to share power with the Dutch in the face of the rising influence of the nationalist middle class of the Republic.

It can be argued that the increasing efforts of the Dutch in the political, military and economic fields constitute a major explanation of the ongoing justification of the Dutch presence in Indonesia. On the one hand, the investments in men and money—including two and a half thousand casualties—demanded a strong moral defence; on the other hand, the Dutch succeeded in regaining the political, military and economic initiative, and felt that each new step forward justified further progression along the same lines. Both the sacrifices and the successes, however limited the latter, constituted major reasons for the continued defence of the Dutch intervention. The ongoing conflict did not eliminate the need for justification but strengthened its ideological basis.

The fact that the military were among the last to accept the end of the empire is readily understandable in view of the strong military attachment to the Dutch position overseas. The conquest of the Indies completed in the nineteenth and early twentieth centuries was almost entirely the achievement of the KNIL, and therefore an important element in the Dutch military heritage.

Moreover, many Dutch military felt responsible for the Indonesian soldiers who served in the colonial army and for that part of the population which had developed ties of friendship with the Dutch. At this point the ideology became rooted in moral feelings of loyalty which changed to guilt at the idea of moving out and thus betraying the Dutch-oriented Indonesians.[35]

It is highly probable that revolutionary wars characterized by a process of escalation and a growing commitment, but without a decisive outcome, engender tenacious loyalties among the men who carry the burden.[36] When the point of no return is reached loyalty and honor will be cited as a last defence against the growing feeling of desperation.

NOTES

[1] Van Doorn and Hendrix, *Ontsporing van geweld: Over het Nederlands/ Indisch/Indonesisch conflict* (Rotterdam: Rotterdam University Press, 1970), ch. II and III, 49 ff., 99 ff.; George McTurnan Kahin, *Nationalism and Revolution in Indonesia* (Ithaca, N.Y.: Cornell U.P., 1952).

[2] H. Colijn, *Koloniale vraagstukken van heden en morgen* (Amsterdam: De Standaard, 1928), 59 ff.

[3] Ch. Kiès, *Het Indonesisch probleem* (Private publication 1948), 12; also Ch. Kiès, *Wat de meeste Nederlanders niet weten omtrent Nederlandsch-Indië* (Deventer: W. van Hoeve, n.d. 1946), 5 ff., 34.

[4] D. J. Jongeneel, *Het spel, dat met Nederlandsch Indië gespeeld wordt* (The Hague: Van Stockum, 1946), 27.

[5] M. van den Heuvel, 'Het Indisch Instructie-Bataljon', *De Militaire Spectator,* Vol. CXVI (1947), 284.

[6] Kahin, *op. cit.,* 351 ff.

[7] *Report of the Parliamentary Commission (States General) Dutch East Indies* (Chairman M. van Poll) (The Hague, May 1946), 23.

[8] Mas Slamet, *Japanese Machinations* (Batavia, February/March 1946), four pamphlets against the Japanese origin of the Indonesian Republic written by a Dutch-oriented Indonesian politician; Jongeneel, *op. cit.,* 31 ff.; C. Gerretson, *Indië onder dictatuur* (Amsterdam and Brussels: Elsevier, 1946), 79; H. W. J. Picard, *De waarheid over Java* (The Hague: Van Hoeve, 1946); *Klare taal: Een bundel radio-redevoeringen van tegenstanders van de overeenkomst van Linggadjati,* with an introduction by W. K. H. Feuilletau De Bruyn (n.d., no publisher, 1947), 17, 21, 23 ff.; P. M. Van Wulfften Palthe, *Psychological Aspects of the Indonesian Problem* (Leiden: E. J. Brill, 1949), 1 ff., 10 ff.; P. S. Gerbrandy, *De scheuring van het rijk: Het drama van de Indonesische crisis* (Kampen: J. H. Kok, 1951), 66-70. Of these authors Gerbrandy was the wartime Dutch prime-minister in London, and several were prominent colonial experts, former colonial senior civil servants, etc.

[9] Of the total force of about 325,000 Japanese in the Indies, no more than 2,000 are assumed to have deserted at the end of the war, some because they had married Indonesian wives. Only part of this category served in the Indonesian army. H. J. Van Mook, *Indonesië, Nederland en de Wereld* (Amsterdam: De Bezige Bij, 1949), 134.   ,

[10] A declaration published in *De Locomótief* (Dutch daily in the East Indies), (29 October, 1949).

[11] Kahin, *op. cit.,* ch. VI and IX.

[12] W. K. H. Feuilletau De Bruyn, *Naar de Sovjet Republiek Indonesia* (1947, 1948, 2nd ed.).

[13] See the publications of Gerretson and Gerbrandy referred to above.

[14] W. Drees, *Zestig jaren levenservaring* (Amsterdam: Arbeiderspers, 1962), 228.

[15] Van Doorn and Hendrix, *op. cit.,* 93 ff.

[16] The present writer's personal experience as a conscripted soldier at the time.

[17] Published in *Van Arnhem tot de Poentjak: Herinneringen aan het 421e Bataljon Garderegiment Prinses Irene. Nederland-Indonesië: Maart 1948-Augustus 1950* (1951), 68 ff.

131

[18]Personal information obtained by the writer at the time.

[19]Radio speech by Major General Buurman van Vreeden (August 1949).

[20]Harry J. Benda, 'Decolonization in Indonesia: The Problem of Continuity and Change', *American Historical Review,* Vol. LXX (1965), 1062 ff.

[21]Kahin, *op. cit.,* 112 ff., 122 ff., 134 ff.

[22]Kahin, *op. cit.,* 292 ff.

[23]Samuel P. Huntington, 'The New Military Politics', in Samuel P. Huntington (ed.), *Changing Patterns of Military Politics* (N.Y.: Free Press of Glencoe, 1962), 30.

[24]See Dutch Government Publication *Nota betreffende het archievenonderzoek naar gegevens omtrent excessen in Indonesië begaan door Nederlandse militairen in de periode 1945-1950* (1949), a memorandum presented by the Prime Minister to the Second Chamber of the Dutch Parliament on 3 June 1949, Supplement 2.

[25]For an extensive analysis of this problem see Van Doorn and Hendrix, *op. cit.,* ch. III and IV.

[26]George Armstrong Kelly, *Lost Soldiers: The French Army and Empire in Crisis 1947-1962* (Cambridge, Mass.: The MIT Press, 1965), 197-99.

[27]Cf. the Dutch public opinion polls on Dutch policy concerning the Indonesian conflict: *De publieke opinie over Indonesië in de jaren 1946-1950,* Newsletter NIPO, No. 1261 (6 February 1969). Arend Lijphart, *The Trauma of Decolonization: The Dutch and West New Guinea* (New Haven and London: Yale U.P., 1966), 122, 125.

[28]Besides Kelly, *op. cit.,* see: John Steward Ambler, *Soldiers against the State: The French Army in Politics* (Garden City, N.Y.: Anchor Books, 1968), Part I and II.

[29]Rob Kroes, 'Decolonization and Military: The Case of the Netherlands', in Morris Janowitz and Jacques van Doorn (eds.), *On Military Intervention* (Rotterdam: University Press, 1971), 93 ff.

[30]Some publications of the Dutch opponents of the official agreement with the Indonesian Republic contained secret information. In 1949 the Head of the Military Intelligence Service (MID), Dr. J. M. Somer, was dismissed because of his secret contacts with political opposition groups in the Netherlands.

[31]Van Doorn and Hendrix, *op. cit.,* 65 ff.

[32]Kroes, *op. cit.* For details of the Indonesian background of naval officers see C. J. Lammers, *Het Koninklijk Instituut voor de Marine* (Assen: Van Gorcum/Prakke & Prakke, 1963), 400 ff.

[33]Charles C. Moskos, Jr., *The American Enlisted Man* (New York: Russell Sage Foundation, 1970), 146 ff.

[34]For instance, the NIRUB (Netherlands Indies Rubber Fund) had ordered production equipment in the United States in 1945 to the value of 48 million Dutch guilders.

[35]The Amboinese soldiers and their families, numbering 12,500 people, were evacuated to the Netherlands. *Ambonezen in Nederland.* Rapport Ministerie Maatschappelijk Werk (The Hague: Government Printing and Publishing Office, 1959), 10 ff.

[36]French observation by Raoul Girardet, 'Civil and Military Power in the Fourth Republic', in Samuel P. Huntington (ed.), *Changing Patterns of Military Politics* (N.Y.: Free Press of Glencoe, 1962), 140.

Chapter 7

USE OF VIOLENCE IN COUNTER INSURGENCY:
THE INDONESIAN SCENE 1945-49

A study of military problems is, in the final analysis, a study of violence. An armed force is, per definition, a potential force for violence; military action is nothing else than the exertion of violence.

In the social sciences this fact is rather frequently overlooked. Studies on military affairs, which now amount to a considerable number, are rarely concerned with actual violence. Sociologists have discussed the military profession and military organization, the relations between army, politics and society, but have often ignored the simple fact that it is impossible to separate these phenomena from the key function of the armed forces.

Even smaller is the number of studies on war atrocities and criminality, generally: on violence in excess. Inspite of a mass of material—particularly on World War II and Vietnam—serious and systematic analysis from the side of the social sciences is lacking.

This chapter is an attempt to lay bare some social conditions which accompanied the use of violence and excessive violence by Dutch troops in counter-insurgency activities in Indonesia in 1945-49. Part of the material is from official documents and publications; part of it has been gathered by the authors* in the years 1948 and 1949 when they were soldiers in the Dutch infantry in Java.

That we talk about violence and excess of violence as two separate categories of phenomena is not fortuitous. This separation can and should be maintained since military performance is limited by rules and regulations. Thus the violation of such norms or regulations is demonstrable.

---

*Jacques van Doorn and William J. Hendrix.

The boundaries cannot sharply be deliniated; neither are they independent of time. Where the boundary is drawn depends on cultural standards, political interests, public opinion and military norms and means. But, however vague this boundary may be, a point can always be indicated where violence turns into excess of violence and the laborious regulation of military action collapses. This chapter will elaborate further on this point—in fact a cloud of points in the frontier region between an act of war and a war crime.

Our purpose is interpretation, not accusation. The facts which are presented here have a place in that explanation; they are not mentioned as facts in themselves. They are elements in a pattern, the results of a social and political process.

CURRENT FICTIONS

Aggressiveness and violence. It is understandable that psychologists particularly have, for a long time, tried to reduce the phenomenon of war to personal aggressiveness, also called a destructive urge. Some authors take their point of departure even from the occurrence of aggression in animals, and subsequently deduce the phenomenon of war from this.[1]

From a sociological point of view, various objections can be brought against this. War is a form of social conflict consisting of the violent clash between organized complexes of men and means, prepared for and adjusted to collective destruction. Forms of aggressive behavior do occur here, but they do not explain the phenomenon; they merely accompany it. To point to the existence of personal aggressiveness is to point to a potency, not to its realization, and certainly not to the institutional conditions under which this realization takes place.

This is not to say that more attention to individual loss of control under war circumstances would not be important. One thing which is conspicuous when one studies the excesses concerned, is the creation of opportunities for personal aggressiveness and the great personal arbitrariness which is possible in some situations. As an experienced officer told us: "out of every one hundred men there are possibly five sadists, and these men now got their opportunities."

Such persons, sometimes coincidentally on the scene, can give free rein to their tendencies. There are many cases to demonstrate what happens.

> The war correspondent Hofwijk has described how a patrol took two prisoners. A discussion arose as to whether or not they should be taken along with the patrol. Some soldiers argued for killing them on the spot because they had been found without uniform in the patrolling regions. Finally they are let free, which causes great frustration with some.[2]
> Varenne, a Dutch conscript soldier, who published a small book about his experiences with war-criminality in Indonesia, mentions a similar affair: "There was a time that two prisoners were taken with us, to point out the road I think; when we turned around the time had come to push these people off. The lieutenant and the scout were not with us; the patrol commander was a sergeant of the reserves, a nice fat guy, a farmer's son . . . he would do the job together with the corporal. When I said he was bloody stupid, because those guys had only been picked up yesterday he let them go good naturedly. This was my only deed of sabotage and it did not take much effort."[3]

Yet these situation sketches are unsatisfactory for those who want a clear insight into the mechanism of violent behavior within the small group. The arbitrariness seems to be total, and this semblance is created because the situation is not sufficiently detailed. There remain many questions to be answered: What does the commander know and do, why don't bystanders interfere, how could the situation become so diffuse, have those directly concerned a special task or do they simply want to square an account? One could continue in this fashion. Violence, certainly excessive violence, does not occur "just like that;" it has a function, or an explanation can be found in institutional disarrangement.

We will now have a closer look at these functions and this disarrangement, guided by two well known perspectives: organizational and situational pressures.

"An order is an order." It is especially in these words that the compelling influence of the military organization and hierarchy on its members' actions has gained notoriety. The expression translates the conception of the army as a "social machine" in terms of absolute personal subordination. It is the clearest definition of the instrumental organizational principle, and it is to this extent directly opposed to the factor of personal arbitrariness we have just discussed.

Departing from the principle of instrumentality one assumes that the soldier translates orders into action "automatically", without imposing any norms himself or without those actions being preceded by any of his own considerations.

The army is then, as it were, punished for keeping intact a one-way traffic system in the command-line: the system operates consistently until right into the region of the absurd and the criminal. If one traces military training in obedience in preceding civil school-systems, resistance seems to be almost excluded.

There is a lot to be said against this seemingly so plausible explanation. In the first place the fact, that no explanation is given here, merely a problemshift. Orders are linking mechanisms, and explaining behavior from given orders is merely pointing to a cause on a higher level. As the military organization is linked in this way until the very top, the causality chain of the events seems to disappear altogether from the organization; we are dealing here with a line of reasoning which brings us to Hitler's "prime mover."

This effect explains a great deal of the popularity of the order-is-order thesis; it is par excellence a way of apologising in the literal meaning of the term.

There are other objections. The idea that military behavior in the field and under wartime conditions stems directly from concrete orders, is a civilian idea which is determined by the fact that only the army of the barracks is visible. Saluting, drill and similar barrack rituals are, indeed, clear expressions of a rigid training in obedience. They are also, however, largely substitutes for factors which determine behavior at the front: because of a lack of these in peace time people have built up an artificial system of controls which disappears into the background in the case of a real armed conflict.

In a situation of war there is no duality of orders given and orders obeyed, but a triangle: threatening danger comes into it. Especially in the highly uncertain situation of guerilla warfare, as in Indonesia, the threat comes from "all around;" one is supposed to take care of oneself and to react according to circumstance.

Civilian observers also frequently underestimate the psychic burden which the exercise of violence imposes, certainly when it is outside the combat situation as such. The average soldier can only with effort meet the order to kill people. When such an order is performed off-hand, then volunteers and "specialists"—e.g. intelligence personnel—are usually involved who have been selected on the basis of a certain toughness.

This is not to say that there have been no concrete orders for hard measures to be taken. Note the Pakisadji case, in August 1947, which involved three Dutch marines who received heavy prison sentences when they refused to burn down part of a village in Eastern Java, since they regarded this as an unjust reprisal. Their commander maintained, as did the Commander-in-Chief, that the safety of the troops made it necessary to remove the village houses.[4]

It is conspicuous that this kind of court martial case rarely occurred, either because commanding officers did not dare to push things too far or because they encountered little resistance. Our own experience is that things were different when the execution of prisoners was concerned: one could refuse this without inviting much trouble.

> We relate here only one case. During a military action in July 1947 (Middle Java), a patrol took a prisoner who had a bullet wound. The man was not seriously wounded but he could not be easily transported. One had the choice between either letting him go or killing him. The commanding non-com officer of the unit decided to do the latter thing and gave the order to a certain soldier. When the latter made it known that he did not like to do this, someone else was ordered. The patrol could then continue.

Situational pressure. Far more widespread and more popular is the thesis that one was caught in a situation which permitted only tough action or aroused "spontaneous" or "unintentional" deeds.

This popularity is understandable. There is again an element of self-justification involved here, in this case not by making others responsible but by transferring the cause—and hence also guilt—to the opponent, or even to something which "nobody could do anything about:" the threatening circumstances, the combat situation or the cruel deeds of the enemy.

Various forms of this mode of explanation can be found varying from reference to the guerilla type of combat and the terror exerted by the enemy to talks about spontaneous reprisals.

> One very often heard of soldiers losing control of themselves when a comrade or commander is killed, in which case "the cowardly assault" is frequently emphasized. Soldiers then go spontaneously into the villages, fire in all directions and take reprisals by burning down dwellings. One later hears commanders then saying that "the troops could not be controlled" because "they were just plain mad."

This may have occurred sometimes, but it is easily exaggerated and very imprecisely described. Collective "spontaneity", even collective action as such, is generally rare; there are almost always those who take the initiative, and these can be kept in hand. The reprisals have often been ordered, in any case aimful, and sometimes planned in advance. They are regarded as military operations.

A quite different form of situational pressure is indicated by the view, that during action in enemy territory one was "lumbered" with prisoners. In the case cited above, described by Hofwijk, the latter says of the two prisoners: "we can't take them with us, nor transport them to a place behind the lines".[5]

Hueting, a psychologist who fought as a soldier in Middle Java and studied his experiences afterwards, has repeatedly referred to this situation. One had to undertake dangerous action with small patrols, sometimes only 15 or 20 men. "When we took prisoners, they were often an embarrassment—what could we do with those people. We could take them with us, but at the cost of our rifle power, since they had to be guarded. And then it was often the case—especially during longer patrols—that we liquidated them." Somewhere else he says: "at a certain moment you can get into a tight spot on patrol. And then you disencumber yourself, to put it somewhat cynically".[6]

This has no doubt happened, but this analysis also leaves the real course of events obscure. It always seems to be the case that "the group" reacts. Just as in the stories about trigger happiness there is, on the verbal level, a dominance of impersonal, collective and non-functional elements in the exertion of violence.

Moreover, in the example given above there is no reference whatsoever to a "spontaneous" reaction; a decision is taken to remain on top of the situation, and this decision is of a rational-tactical character, not an irrational-reactive one.

Something similar holds for the frequently occurring tough interrogations of prisoners military units take during a mission. The argument is then, that the group as a whole is in a situation of emergency and therefore has to obtain, as quickly as possible, information about the situation on the spot.

In itself this is correct. The argument, however, does not explain why most prisoners are taken first to the company's headquarters and that only there are they submitted to a hard interrogation, hence at the point that the emergency situation no longer exists. So the relation between excess of violence and danger is not direct, as some participants would like to suggest, but indirect: under difficult circumstances certain commanders try to maintain control of a region by drastic action.

To get a grip with the phenomenon of violence a far more precise analysis is necessary. Even when there seems, at first sight, to be a spontaneous reaction, complicating factors are involved which can often hardly be observed by participants. Let us give an example of this.

A patrol was sent from a platoon's camp in Middle Java to an unsafe area. In a village there the *tjarik* (local administrative official) was asked whether the *tentara* (Indonesian army) had been seen, but he denied this.
Subsequently the patrol left the village and began crossing a river bed that had largely fallen dry. In the course of this two soldiers moved slightly ahead of the platoon. When they were in the middle of the river bed a group of Indonesian guerillas began firing from the other side. One of the soldiers fell down, wounded; the other one dropped down and fired back. The other members of the patrol were firing over them to the other side. Then the wounded man was brought back to the platoon position, meter by meter, and an emergency bandage is applied. A small group was sent to the company's headquarters to get help. After a while the firing stops.
The soldier, M., was wounded in three places, twice in the chest. He was bleeding heavily but was not in a condition of shock; he was fully conscious. He was reported as having regretted that he could not go on.
Meanwhile a doctor carrying blood serum and the company commander arrived. According to information received from the group the commander was with M. when his condition quickly worsened. The commander allegedly said: "M., boy, keep your pecker up; we'll get your revenge".
After this the unit goes into the village. The village police, about 15 men, were gathered together. Again the question was asked whether the *tentara* had been seen. Despite threats the villagers continued to say that they knew nothing. After this one of the men was shot dead; another one had to carry away the corpse. He too maintained that he had not seen any guerillas and was also shot. Then the company commander intervened and prevented any further executions. Meanwhile village dwellings were set on fire and at least 80 went up in flames.

The story, released in this fashion, seems entirely watertight. A patrol loses a man because the village people—who are formally obliged to report—have kept silent about guerillas they must have known were there. The commander, regarded as a very humane officer, reacts violently at the instant that the soldier lies dying at his feet. The comrades of the dead men start to take revenge; the officer can stop the executions but the burning of houses goes on.

However, going deeper into the affair, one learns that the man who interrogated the two members of the village-police and killed them, was an Indonesian henchman of the units' intelligence group. This man, just as the other members of the intelligence group, must have felt that the "alarm system", guaranteed by this group, had failed. It is also significant that after the clash the soldiers did not turn against the guerillas on the other side of the river, but against the village. For the intelligence unit it was mainly the village people who were held responsible.

Those who later heard of the affair, could not believe that the officer present had ordered the reprisals. Moreover, it is not clear from the report whether or not such an order had in fact been given. It is possible that the commander's attitude was tacitly supporting this action, but it is equally probable that the intelligence group and the soldiers acted for him.

It may even be doubted whether he spoke the words to the dying soldier that were ascribed to him. They fitted however in the justification post factum.

When the picture is surveyed a combination of factors can be seen in which "spontaneous revenge" seems to be the dominant motive—and this indeed does play a role—but in which also certain individuals are taking the initiative and others yield to this, which determines the course of events.

The rationalizing character of this kind of explanation becomes very much more outspoken, when one translates the concept of "situation" to the whole of the guerilla. The military command and the politicians responsible in particular take this line to demonstrate the "inevitability" of excesses.

This holds for the general suggestion implied in the frequently made assertion that the Dutch troops behind the demarcation (cease-fire) lines were provoked to the utmost. The Governer General, Hubertus van Mook, thought that "it would be easy to understand that the continuous attacks of the Indonesians had a very provoking effect on our troops. They were confined within narrow boundaries, like a bear on a rope, and continuously baited by bystanders who knew that they would be safe beyond these boundaries."[7]

This is, however, only partly true. It is true to the extent that such fighting tactics put an extra psychic burden on the troops, impose heavy responsibilities on commanders, especially those on the lower levels, and make control over what is happening very difficult. It is, however, for the greater part untrue because it was not "the troops" that were provoked, but professional officers who knew that military success was within their reach but who were hampered in achieving this by the political negotiations and the tactical moves of the enemy.

The guerilla type of warfare does, indeed, explain a lot. But this explanation should not be couched in terms of reactive violence on the part of individual soldiers, but in terms of a reactive organization of violence by the higher levels of command. The trying of Indonesian prisoners of war by special military courts, the tolerance of a widely spread, uncontrolled, hard police-regime, and the use of Special Forces with far-reaching powers—that was the "reaction" to the impossibility of closing off the demarcation lines and ending the guerilla warfare. The answer to the situation was formulated at the highest level; the ranks were ordered to implement it.

THE ARMED FORCES IN COMMAND

War is regarded as constituting an abnormal social situation, an interregnum between two periods of normality. During this interregnum only one institution is able to function, i.e., the armed forces. It is even specially devised and arranged "to cope with" the war and it assumes control while other institutions withdraw. Legitimate order is suspended; specialists appear on the scene.

In the past the army's scope of action remained nevertheless limited to the front. Only at the front where it met the enemy forces, were the exceptional rules of war completely valid. Now the war has become "total", the front is "everywhere".

In Indonesia, similarly, the role of the army was not limited to "the front;" there was, in fact, no front, only a preliminary cease-fire line and a partial occupation—the result of an agreement over the cease-fire—which could be easily infiltrated. The situation in the country as a whole, moreover, was such that a more or less disguised military administration was deemed necessary. Dutch troops did, indeed, spend more energy on maintaining "law and order" than on real military action against a regular army.

This kind of occupation implies that the military cannot limit itself to confrontation with the enemy along a narrow front—"the thin red line"—but is involved with the enemy and with its own side in virtually all sectors of social life. Instead of functioning as a violence-producing apparatus, it develops into a broadly implemented administrative machine. It functions, in fact, as a substitute for civilian authority.

Beginning at the top of the political system, it can be established that the Dutch government at the Hague put an armed force at the disposal of the government—the Governor-General—of the Dutch East Indies. Once it arrived there, control over this army by political circles in Holland became more loose than was probably desired. Not only the geographical distance involved contributed to this, but also the formal division of powers between the Dutch and the Dutch East Indies governments as far as direct responsibility for military affairs was concerned.

A clear demonstration of the impotence of the Hague can be found in efforts made by the Dutch Parliament and the Minister for Overseas Territories to obtain information about the excesses ascribed to the troops in Indonesia. A government memorandum of 1969, analyzing the steps taken by the Hague, described the situation in succinct but significant terms.[8]

The request by a number of parliamentarians to instigate an independent inquiry "by a commission of persons not subordinated to military or administrative authorities in Indonesia" (at the time Dutch East Indies) was advised against by the Minister for Overseas Territories. Only after repeated urgings from Parliament did the Minister undertake a cautious step by requesting the so-called High Representative of the Crown (successor of the Governor-General)—it was meanwhile 1949, a year after the first requests in Parliament—"to inform him whether the latter would appreciate it if some lawyers were sent, to set up, *under the guidance of the High Representative* (sic!), a non-judicial inquiry into the character and scope of the excesses committed and the measures taken against them" (italics are ours—J.v.D.).

The request was granted, but by putting personal pressure on the Minister the High Representative managed to impose his conditions be limited to cases which had already been brought to the attention of the government. Not only the requested independence of the commission but also the breadth of their frame of reference was successfully staved off by the East Indies government.

At the end of October 1949 the commission left for Indonesia. It returned two months later. The report, which was signed only by two of the three members, was limited to the South Celebes affair. It was finished only in 1954 and then disappeared into the ministerial desk.[9]

The interwovenness of military and civil interests and institutions does not only hold as far as the administration of justice is concerned. It is a general characteristic of the forces which as a "total institution" possess in virtually every field a high degree of autonomy—a consequence of the internal completeness of the apparatus. The armed forces have not only their own bakeries and transport branches, but also their own press, schools, information and intelligence services, their own police-formations and legal courts.

This holds for a military regime but also for a state of martial law, as it existed in Indonesia. The network of military positions and relations went right through the whole society, from the top, direct under the highest government authority, to remote outposts, where the commanders of small military units could afford to put pressure on village heads, to create special police units, to arrest civilians and keep them temporarily imprisoned, to exercise censorship, gather and use political information, to requisition labor, burn down buildings for tactical reasons, etc.

A few sentences of a patrol report can indicate how simply things were handled. We quote below some randomly selected reports of patrols of the 3rd Batallion, 7th Infantry Regiment which had been stationed in a Middle Java region east of Semarang, near the cease-fire line.

Report of a patrol of 13 November 1947: "In connection with the kidnapping of a Chinese near village D. we searched the village and took 10 male persons with us to company headquarters with the purpose of obtaining information."

Report of a patrol on 3 December 1947: "We took 80 men with us from village B. for interrogation in T. The population of the villages S. and W. had already fled."

Report of a patrol on 6 December 1947: "We arrested 25 male persons from B. and brought them to VV. for further interrogation. We found a new *markas* (Indonesian platoon's headquarters) the walls of which were covered with the most obscene and disgusting remarks addressed to the Dutch troops. We destroyed these by setting fire to it."

These patrols had a strength of between 25 and 35 men and were commanded by a sergeant. There was little correction or control of this obvious concentration of power. The military "closed ranks" in any case as the outside world was concerned. Even marginal figures, such as the military chaplains, put themselves behind the hierarchy and exerted only internal criticism, if any.

What occurred at the highest level, also occurred at the lowest, but more obscurely. In fact, there too the system of "military administration" was operative. Control of a territory presupposed more than military action: it constituted, at least in intention, a striving for complete social control, being based on a highly personal interpretation of the bringing about of law and order by all means.

Seen in this way, the lowest hierarchical level, represented by local commanders—often lieutenants and sergeants—had at the same time the character of military, civil and legal administration, but all in an improvised fashion.

Even the lowest echelons of the native civil service—the village heads and district chiefs—were involved in military responsibilities and, in a way, pushed into an impossible position. Their line of communication with the Dutch civil administration was cut off by the imposition of military duties about which they had sworn to silence. In the efforts of the Indonesian guerilla to attack the Dutch system of control they became the first victims. Hundreds of them were murdered, thousands more were physically molested.

Rather than a story of strength, this all constitutes a tale of weakness. The Dutch government at the Hague left things to the Netherlands East Indies government; the East Indies government was inclined to leave things to the armed forces; the army provided a military administration, the implementation of which was left to the lower commanders; these commanders had soldiers available whom, however, they had to use for police and intelligence tasks. The types of violence, resulting from this situation, will be discussed now.

TYPES OF VIOLENCE

The artificiality of the barracks. There are many sociological studies of army barracks. They agree in their descriptions of a closed, strongly hierarchical and very formal organization which serves primarily to make a citizen a soldier; for this reformation there is a whole arsenal of regulations and manipulations, rituals and symbols, practices and exercises, together creating a pattern of behavior which distinguishes the soldier from the civilian. The minute regulation of almost all behavior is conducive to a situation in which the individual soldier quickly finds his way around and becomes involved in the social machinery of the barracks army.

Though the army is in its basic function, and therefore also in the contents of its training, different from all other social institutions, this difference is less great than is often, on the basis of mere externalia, presumed. The modern army constitutes a modern organization.

The norms of efficiency and rationality on which military organization is based do not deviate from those of any other big institution. Expertise and devotion to duty are demanded, achievement is rewarded and negligence punished, the attempt is made to motivate the individual members, they are led and their behavior is controlled; army training possesses virtually all the traits of a schooling process which is already familiar to the newly recruited soldier; instructors, lessons, exercises and sanctions.

The "ordinary character" of the barracks is brought out even more by the intricacy and autonomy of its organization, where many functions are little different from those in civilian society. The army has its technical and clerical staff, postal services and hospitals, its bridge building and telegraphy, its gymnasiae and recreation halls. More and more soldiers are becoming concerned with "civilian" tasks, and increasingly less so with "specific" battle tasks.

These latter tasks have numerous special forms as well. The technical services, such as the artillery, engineering corps, signal corps, etc., require primarily a certain degree of professional knowledge and only secondarily an orientation towards dealing with "the enemy". The use of cannon, radar installations and radio sets constitutes a vital part of military operations, but, rather than the old physical military capabilities this requires technical knowledge and skills which, because of orders from above and because of the orientation of the techniques concerned, have a military effect.

The first consequence of this fact is that a soldier involved in these functions is a soldier more in the "objective" than in the "subjective" sense. Or, put in a different way: whereas the result of his actions is related to the massive exertion of violence, his involvement in this violence is secondary. Remote control renders the enemy invisible; the soldier is in wartime possibly in danger, but this danger has as impersonal and mechanical a character as he presents himself for the enemy.

A second important consequence is that he can realistically train in peacetime; as far as its technical aspects are concerned, the training situation is not very different from a wartime situation. A war pilot, an artilleryman, or a member of the navy is in many ways the product of his training. Under real war circumstances he can fail in morale, but as a technician of violence he only has to do what he has been taught to do many times before in similar or simulated circumstances.

Thirdly, the soldier in the technical services is to an increasing degree "functionally autonomous;" if he knows his trade, then his commander is only a man who orders him to make use of his skills, at what time and against which targets—and even this latter aspect is now mechanized in the most modern weapons: the anti-aircraft missile itself searches for the target.

Though the trend is in the same direction as far as the non-technical branches of the services are concerned, there is here a fundamentally different situation. The infantryman—still the "typical" soldier—is also taught the command of a number of manipulations. He is taught to control his weapons in the same school-like fashion and is tried out in exercises of various types. Firearms, especially automatic small arms, as far as their handling is concerned, come close in a number of ways to the weapons which are used by the more technical branches of the services. The soldier's distance to his physical enemy increases.

But the fact remains that that physical enemy is the target of his military actions. That enemy is visible and is generally a visible threat. The infantryman approaches him not from a position protected by technical devices but is moving in a field in which he, as his enemy, must try to fit in as best as possible. His confrontation with the enemy amounts to a confrontation with an armed man. To train for this confrontation implies an absolute breach with the civilian past. The profession of infantrymen does not exist outside the army; civilian continuity with the past is disrupted by the army.

At the same time this infantry training can never be made fully realistic. One can try to imitate reality by low fire and dangerous maneuvers, but the training situation is always far removed from the reality of the war as the infantryman encounters it. It is for him especially that the words of the war reporter Erny Pyle hold: "Say what you will, nothing can make a complete soldier except battle experience."[10]

His relation to the commander is connected with this. The commander is, given the task of the infantryman, much more than a mere superior: he functions as combat leader, as "guide" in a dangerous situation of real combat. He must have the confidence of his men and the certainty that they will follow him.

Again the barracks situation can not fully imitate this relation. Therefore the commander appears, necessarily, as a hierarchical superior, as a technical superior, as the person who implements sanctions, but not in his essential role as combat leader. As is the situation itself of the infantryman, so is the position of the commander in the training period an artificial one.

This artificiality greatly reinforces the formalism of a peacetime army. The total structure of ritual and rules serves to a high degree to hide the artificial function of the army, or even its lack of a real function. Hierarchy and discipline function as substitutes for the challenge exerted by the reality of war. Great distance between cadre (esp. officers) and men is the main consequence of this.

Thus the infantryman experiences the barracks situation mainly as a training in obedience not only in the formal sense—"an order is an order"—but also in the factual sense of being reduced to obedience, because of the impossibility of undertaking something himself and because of the conviction that those "up there" know better and "can bloody well do what they like."

This separation between cadre and ranks implies at the same time a difference in normative integration, that is to say to the extent to which the specific norms and obligations of the wartrade constitute a substitute regulation of conduct for what people have left behind in their now useless civilian norms. Briefly indicated, this difference amounts to the fact that an officer is familiar with some ideas regarding the normative limitations of the use of violence, which he can use as criteria for his decisions, whereas for the soldier obedience has to suffice. He knows that the norms of civilian life no longer apply: these are not replaced, however, by military norms but by a relation of dependence.

Thus an army encounters war. In the top layer of the army are those responsible for the whole, who are, at least to a certain extent, conscious of the obligation of controlling the potential violence available as well as possible. At the bottom there are, besides the technicians of violence and the supporting services, the many soldiers who are confronted by the challenge without really knowing it and without directions regarding the limits to which they should feel bound. For them—and for many of their commanders—the reality of violence comes as a shock.

From this shock—originating in the clash between its own exertion of violence and that of the enemy—emerges the fighting army. It is a product of barracks training only to the extent to which the barracks provides an organizational framework and technical skills; the soldier is provided with a commander and with a weapon. But for the infantryman the real use of this weapon only starts with combat itself. What kinds of soldiers and what kinds of commanders come into being is a matter of combat experience.

To put it summarily: the army defines the computable potential in violence: the real character of violence is defined by the combat situation. Therefore the special character of violence engendered under special war circumstances will constitute our point of departure in the further analysis of the real functioning of the army.

Technical violence. A very specifically technical branch of the services is the engineer corps. The publications of members of this corps who served in Indonesia are revealing this. They are written in the spirit of tradesmen and engineers who are proud to see their technical projects come about under the most difficult circumstances of material, aids and appliances, and environment. They are technical all-rounders and almost create the impression of being irritated by the armed activity around them, which prevents them from achieving even more rapid and beautiful technical results.[11]

The engineer corps is, however, an auxiliary technical corps; it does not produce technological violence. This does not hold for the navy, the airforce, the artillery and the tank corps. Contrary to the practice of the auxiliary technical corps, they produce considerable direct violence. It is dehumanized because it is mechanical violence, an adumbration of our modern civilization, because it is, at the same time, calculable and almost effortlessly successful.

These are modern branches because their use requires little manpower; those who manipulate them are few, those who become the victims many. Often the target is not even directly visible; the firing is based on the observations of others, who provide map-coordinates or a situation sketch. This holds very clearly for the actions of the airforce, but coastal bombardments by the navy are often also performed in this fashion.

Artillery and tanks are nearer to the enemy; they are moreover in the field and run a greater risk of being involved in a direct personal confrontation with their opponent. Tanks and armoured cars are most endangered, and for fire contact at a short distance they need specially supporting infantry, apart from mine-sweeping crews which have to clear the road.

The thing which interests us is the sort of violence involved here. The targets are often only roughly indicated: terror bombings by planes to lame the adversary's morale or tanks which come tearing along with shrieking sirens trying to chase away an—invisible— enemy, with bursts of fire from their machine guns.

But where the firing is better aimed the targets are only in a derived sense human; often positions, bunkers and entrenchments are involved, sometimes concentrations of the enemy. Not "the others" form the target, but "the positions" and "the entanglements" of the others.

Below follows an example of the role which the airforce (LSK) played in the advance during the Second Police Action (Middle-Java, December 1948).[12]

Use of artillery in advance during First Police Action (West Java, 1947): "For this a great number of fire concentrations were prepared, of which some were to be given according to a 'time schedule;' others on demand. Further support by a creeping barrage was projected for 3-6 RVA (field artillery). This creeping barrage followed the route of the Postweg-highway in such a way that the positions which covered the road from both sides fell under it. It had 33 lines, was 150 m. wide, going ahead 50 m. per minute;

the number of shots per line was 2 per piece per minute. Hence a fire density of $1.5 \times 0.5 \times 8 \times 2 = 12$ shots per hectare ($= +/- 2$ acres). Aided by a model of the Postroad and environment the course of the supporting creeping barrage could be established."[13]

Concerning the use of tanks in the advance "it is recommended to also consider the battering qualities of a tank. Machine gunners near and on the advance-road can, when they open fire at a short distance, be battered and driven under foot. Not very thick trees, in which there are snipers, can be ridden to the ground and bamboo-wooden or light stone houses can be pushed in."

As far as operations in the city are concerned "defenders with low morale will flee when some tanks approach firing, which on flat streets can result in some hits as well. The shrieking of the tanks and sirens can even cause a panic at this stage."[14]

During the Second Action the above procedure was applied exactly in this fashion.

Advance from:	Day and hour + bombing line, i.e., a line which the troops should not cross at the hour mentioned:	To be bombed or machine-gunned by LSK (names of villages)
Bodja	Day A	
	(1) hour U line NW-ZO Goenoeng Sidjamboel (7687) (departure from SQ-line the day before from Limbangan (8193)— Bodja (8099)	Telegapoetjang (7685) Dringo (7685) Wonosan (7586) Karangtengah (7485)
	(2) hour U + 4 hours line NS through hpt 824 (7486)	Rowo (7385) Rowoseneng (7386)
	(3) hour U + 10 hours line NS through Westside kpg Rowo (7385)	Delok (7183) Kandangan (7082)
	(4) hour U + 12 hours line EW through G. Siloeing (7285)	Delok (7183) Kandangan (7082)
	(5) hour U + 16 hours line EW southside kpg Kandangan (7082)	Sendang (7282) Sidaredja (6977) Temanggoen (6975)

All three of these examples concern the use of the more technical branches of the services during the Police Actions. This was not fortuitous. The counter-guerilla which flared up after this, offered far fewer opportunities for these branches; the continuous mopping-up actions in the occupied territory were more laborious.

"After having obtained our own territory" so somebody signs in a publication by an artillery unit "the specific artillery character which had characterized the work of the regiment thus far, was lost."[15]

This held, to a certain extent, for the other arms of the services as well. Their significance was based on their great fire power and their wide range of possible use. A tank squadron or a navy vessel have no fixed base; they can be directed to wherever their support is required. What was required in the counter guerilla, however, was extensive information regarding the field, inclusive of the population. Successful control of a region was based primarily on knowledge regarding that region; one had to stay there for a long time, one had to be "at home" there. An artillery man or a tank unit member is, per definition, however, a stranger. Neither the population nor the enemy personally concern him.

This is made beautifully clear by the above examples. These are war orders but they could as well be excerpts from a program for maneuvers. The "bombing line", the "creeping barrage" and the "battering capacity" of the tank constitute technical characteristics of the military system, which retain their significance without a real enemy being present.

The pilot, the artillery man, even the tank crew rarely see anything of the consequences of their actions; a follow-up report, or intermediate observations (air reconnaissance) must inform him, and that sort of information is bloodless. If he sees anything at all, then it is a shell burst, an explosion, a pillar of fire, a plume of smoke. Members of a tank crew we talked with told us they had participated in many missions in Indonesia but did not have any clear notion of the effect of their actions in terms of victims.

The limited value of these weapons in counter-guerilla action has not impeded their frequent use. Insiders told us that they could only take for granted that in these actions many victims were civilians. The limited discriminatory capacity of these weapons added to the facts of a frequently high population density and of an adversary taking cover among this population, made this very probable indeed.

One single example. On the 16 January 1949 the *Kampong* (village) Penanggoenang in Middle-Java was bombed by a few Dutch planes. Since in this region a plane had once been shot down and the presence of strong detachments of the Indonesian army was presumed, this mountainous *kampong* was chosen as a target. What was not known was the fact that in this village 340 Chinese were being held by the Indonesians. The bombing led to a catastrophe: 41 Chinese were killed and 59 wounded. The mistake resulted in a very thorough inquiry and one wonders whether this would have also been undertaken if the victims had been Indonesian citizens. The documents merely mention that one should presume that the "well-disposed elements" among the population had fled before the bombing commenced.[16]

It is also conspicuous that heavy weapons were used when there was a dearth of infantry. Artillery men complained that these actions were not well thought out. So for instance in West Java: "Often artillery fire on *kampongs* or covered parts of the field was demanded after resistance was encountered, or information obtained about the (probable) presence of enemy concentrations, but the firing was not followed up by infantry action."

How this should be done the authors of this particular piece describe by taking a case in which the army wanted to drive out a group of 10-15 people from a *kampong*: an artillery barrage on the *kampong* without the *kampong* being searched is the answer. "If there was not enough infantry to search through a *kampong* or a covered part of the field, or if it was undesirable to do so, the target was closed off and surrounded by machine gun fire. After this artillery drove the enemy with advancing fire out of the *kampong* and into the machine gun fire. This method was applied successfully."[17]

The style of arguing here and the technical jargon is, in general, characteristic of the technical weapons. One develops "methods" for belaboring an "object", one gains experience and draws conclusions, which are translated into improved methods "the enemy" remains an abstraction; he is the guinea pig in the operation, which is regarded as being an experiment in which there is room for improvement.

The same technical attitude can be found in descriptions of landing operations of the marines in East Java. From the reports one gains the impression that these were also undertaken to at last make use of the opportunity for a "real" landing operation, though the military necessity was not evident. These reports are dominated by the cheerful, tone of professionals who, without running too much risk themselves, had gained an interesting experience.

We stress here the same point we started with: these troops, and especially their commanders, did not view their actual combat experience as being non-concomitant with their training period: one certainly now had to work under heavier conditions, there was also real danger, but the various parts functioned according to plan and that plan had been prepared in advance.

Finally it should be noticed that, given this disposition, it was not thought possible that the use of these weapons could lead to excesses. Though the army was operating amidst a civilian population, and—as we saw above—using such weapons as air attacks, artillery or tank shelling, etc., and though these actions were undertaken in densely populated places, there is no talk anywhere of "excesses." The psychic distance from "the enemy," an abstract entity for the technician of violence, obviously impedes awareness of the fact that something more than making "mistakes" could happen. These latter events were regrettable but inevitable. "From chipping comes chips."

It is often remarked that if the people in the Vietnamese village Song My had not been killed by an infantry unit but wiped out by the airforce, the affair would never have reached the public. The judgement on the Dutch actions in Indonesia confirms this. The Government Report of 1969 only contains individual deeds of violence; the affects of technical weapons were not taken into consideration.[18]

Obviously there are various kinds of excesses and some kinds are not drawn into the discussion. They are not the consequence of an individual derailment by soldiers in the field, but of technical destruction systems, use of which is ordered from higher up. The distinction made confirms the tendency to shift responsibility to the bottom of the organization. The Dutch Government also did this.

Infantry violence. The nature of the infantry as such does not exclude functional organization. The Special Forces formula constitutes, to a great extent, an attempt to create such an organization: in such units the formal-bureaucratic structure of the barracks army is substituted by the formation of a number of combat units with great autonomy, responsible only to higher commanders.

In these units the distinction between commanding officers and men is much less than is the case in "normal" military units. The commander is here really a combat leader; he is the leader of his men and must, in order to maintain himself, excell in the same capacities characterizing his men. However great his power, relations here are—though it may sound strange—more "democratic" than in the rest of the army, because the group members have dangerous missions and operate in small units or even individually; in this way they have access to operational plans and to knowledge which normally remains inaccessible to those in the lowest echelons of military organization. For the "commando" the transition from training to front situation is also less. His training is carefully tuned to realistic circumstances and hence is tougher and more dangerous. In selection as well as in specialization he anticipates the real exertion of violence. When regarded in this way the group constitutes a "weapon" in the technological sense.

All this does not hold to the same extent for the "normal" infantry which is, in the barracks, treated with more consideration because of political and humanitarian pressures. The normal GI only experiences violence in combat circumstances, which he "recognizes," to be sure, from his training period but which he only learns to "manipulate" in the course of combat. The main element in this manipulation is the confusing and threatening presence of an armed opponent.

The barracks army changes into a combat army because of confrontation with such an opponent. The norms change and, with these, mutual appreciation and the appreciation for one's own skills and daring. Displays of "masculinity" and "toughness" are now revealed as shows which could be kept up during group-games in the barracks, but are now meaningless. People are frightened and they are not afraid of admitting this. The dare-devil, the "stunt-man" who likes to pose as a hero, is submitted to criticism, he endangers the situation of the others.

Our platoon, which, interalia, was closely observed by us on this point, showed the change-over clearly and rapidly. Even after the first few days following its arrival in Indonesia (1947), when the platoon was guarding a military camp of tents at the edge of Jakarta, the process of mutual reappreciation began. People who had played a dominating role in the barracks turned out to prefer being on guard duty with two men, which made the time they were on duty increase but their fear decrease. Others, who previously had hardly been taken seriously, emerged as cool and confident persons, who performed their lonely duty without hesitation.

Officers too did not escape from this process of reappreciation according to new norms. The insecurity and the threat which is offered by the situation in the field separates the individualists from the bureaucrats; those who are enamoured by cheap successes and the dedicated.

This process of reselection continued during the whole duration of service, until and including the last heavy period when some who had kept up their courage until then gave up, and others finally got the chance to show what they were really worth.[19]

Here too a differentiation could be made, especially between those soldiers serving in the cities and those serving at the outposts. The former hardly experienced this process of selection. They remained naive about the phenomenon of violence and towards the Indonesians whom they never encountered as "opponents" and whom they never came to know from nearby. Their attitude was redolent of that of the members of the technical services: impersonal in their relation to the other party.

The phenomenon of violence—which interests us here—is found in the guerilla war. In accordance with this the reapplication of personalities and attitudes is based on the success (or otherwise) of counter-guerilla techniques.

In newly recruited troops reactions are often panicky and uncoordinated. There is a period in which people "shoot at everything that moves" and in which this order is given by commanders who are just as unsure of themselves as their troops. This is a period of mistakes and errors, which sometimes leads to the making of victims amidst the civilian population.

People gradually gain in experience, but to an insufficient degree. Too few troops move over too extensive an area. One has to passively endure the activities of snipers along the communication routes; one is always wrong when one tries to find the guerilla fighters among the population. In short: the infantry fails in a situation for which it has not been trained and with which it cannot cope.

Different reactions to this situation can be observed. Firstly there is acquiescence, a reaction which especially troops in relatively safe regions can afford; they perform their routine patrols and leave things as they are. The "working over" of the region they leave to specialists: the politically operating intelligence groups which keep things "under control" with the aid of Indonesian henchmen and their own alarm system. Another way of reacting, which can predominate in dangerous areas, is "hitting back" in a wild and aimless way. Revenge is taken for the activities of snipers; one starts shooting at all those who flee and all those who appear "suspicious", one tries to obtain information by dilettantly executed pressure on the population.

> From a personal report by a war volunteer (West Java): "Another form of action was killing to set an example." When a patrol tried in vain to find enemies and weapons in a suspected village, about which information had been obtained, the population was chased out of their houses and induced to give further information. This was often useless partly because the population feared reprisals partly because it sympathized with the Republic. In such cases after repeated threats, some poor bastards would be taken out of the row, stiff with fear, thrown to the ground, with a gun on his breast and, after the warning that this would be the fate of the rest of the population if people did not want to talk, shot. This measure was also useless, of course. The village head would be ordered to bury the corpse and the patrol continued.

A good example of a tough reprisal measure, stemming from impotence, is provided by the following case, which occurred in Middle Java in the period just after the Second Police Action (January 1949). We give this case here in detail with some background information.

> In the region concerned considerable infiltration had taken place; especially the main road, was under heavy pressure from the guerillas. Between points X and Y a "death road" had come about which could only be partly controlled until post Z. Another part went through an area, which, as a consequence of previous fighting, was depopulated.

> In the environment of this road—in a hilly and thinly populated region— remnants of a strong enemy formation were operating which probably had about several hundred killed. The Dutch troops had had seven killed and a number of wounded because of attacks by this formation. Their opponents were well-armed (automatic firearms and hand-grenades). Virtually all the Dutch killed had strange wounds which were ascribed to the use of dum-dum bullets.

> At the end of January a supply waggon was shot at near X—a place within a region which was under Dutch control again and in which the population had returned. The driver was killed instantly; inside the truck one soldier was mortally wounded—he died a quarter of an hour later—and one Indonesian female washer. About eight persons were wounded in total.

> Inside the driver's cabin there were, in addition to the driver, two other soldiers. One was wounded in both knees the other one only hurt by glass

fragments. When the truck started to swerve this last soldier grabbed the wheel, shoved the dead driver aside and drove out of the danger region until, about five kilometers from X, the engine stopped.

Soldier B who had at first tried to give some help to the wounded left the truck and started running towards X, got hold of a bicycle on the way and warned the first post in X. Immediately a counter-action was undertaken but without result. The dead and wounded were transported to X, the wounded later to Y.

In Z, 25 prisoners had been taken during a "mopping up" action. Twenty-one of these were taken with a patrol and the ID from Z to where the ambush had taken place and there shot dead. Eye witnesses from the patrol state that the brigade-commander from X was present and that a prisoner was ordered to put those who were shot against the hill from which the snipers had been shooting. After this he was to have been freed.

At the place of the ambush a wooden cross was erected.

Some members of the force occupying Z saw the place a few days after. There was a penetrating smell of decomposing bodies. The intelligence group of Z alleged that the population made a detour of many miles (this was a trade-route) to avoid the spot.

Those concerned were of the opinion that the prisoners had mainly been civilians, who had been taken from the surrounding villages during the mopping up action after the attack on Z. At first there was little criticism of this reprisal measure. Later some showed contempt for it. There was talk of "nazi-methods." The insecurity of the road decreased after this incident, but still continued to exist for months for the same reasons as the "take-over" by the guerillas had originally taken place: a lack of Dutch troops.

It is clear, that in such cases there was an abuse of military violence. Traditional military and police ethics were inoperative here; the commanders stepped out of line. The army, taken as an institution of more or less controlled violence does not function in such cases; it produces "uncontrolled" violence.

Yet this way of reacting was not general. A great number of cases can be cited in which such reprisals did not occur. It was often the attitude and personality of the commander which was decisive. In the troops too support for such measures was—as appears from the second example mentioned—not general. The war volunteer quoted earlier started to resist these methods and was then boycotted.

This picture of different attitudes, differentiated according to person, is, however, far less interesting than the also-present functional differentiation. We mean by this the fact that in each unit there were, besides commanders and "normal" troops, specialists in violence on the one hand and, on the other, peripheral figures often without a real combat function (signal men, medical aid soldiers). Whereas the former, during the training period or in the field, were characterized by "toughness," the latter often took a distance towards this kind of thing.

Even in a short clash with the enemy this diversity of attitudes could come out. Hofwijk describes a patrolling platoon which suddenly found a number of *Hizbullah* (members of an Islamic military force) trapped in a valley, from which they could be shot at from a higher point.

Everyone is excited. Several of the enemy run for cover; one is shot down. Hofwijk observes: "One soldier makes a little notch in the hilt of his gun. And behind me, unarmed as I am, there is a guy with a radio set who has been walking the whole morning with a heavy load on his shoulders and who is now swearing: 'Man, man. . . . what a world . . . oh (swearing again) what a world! They're making notches in the hilt of their gun.' Another soldier fills the magazine of his machine gun: 'Emptied two' he says with content 'yesterday two of our boys . . . how do you like this shooting gallery . . . great isn't it?'."[20]

Besides this "negative" selection there is a positive one: An example of the latter is the case of the sniper, who is added to many "skirmishing" units as a specialist. He belongs to the category of semi-commandos, destined for specially heavy tasks, technically and personally a separate figure:

Van Heek describes how he gets into difficulties with his patrol when one of his men is heavily wounded and they are far from their bivouac. "It was now essential not to be ambushed on the way back, because the patrol group had become far too vulnerable. At a distance I could see through my binoculars suspect persons creeping through the rice fields to position themselves along our possible route. I avoided the most obvious road however, went zig-zagging through the field and gave the order to shoot at all suspicious persons who did not obey our order to come closer. The sniper attached to our unit, who with his special gun could shoot extremely accurately within distances of one thousand meters, was kept very busy. Walking cross country and wading through the rivers gave, however, a lot of difficulty in transporting our wounded man. He suffered terrible pain but did not utter a sound. After hours of hard work we finally reached, late in the afternoon, our bivouac."[21]

This short sketch provides a clear insight into the mechanism: the group as a whole is vulnerable, driven into a corner. The commander especially feels responsible for the wounded man. It is he who through his field glasses—a "technical" advantage over his men—can observe and appreciate the situation, and who has the competence to issue the hard order which should see the patrol safely home. The main executor is the sniper who, owing to his special gun, is the man who can successfully fulfill this order. The other members of the group play a secondary role.

This incident clearly illustrates a situation which one encounters again and again. Violence—the order for it and its execution—is in the hands of small numbers. Not "the troops" act or react, but certain members, often commanders, often specialists.

"The situation" in which a combat unit finds itself or "the mood" prevailing in such a unit are of course important in the explanation of what takes place when violence and its derailment occur. But precise analysis of the incidents reveals that "that situation" or "that mood" is mainly relevant for the decisive actions of single individuals.

This is in essence the same phenomenon as has been noted in studies of revolutionary or criminal mass behavior. It is the masses who determine the psychic climate, but it is often individuals—often of a certain calibre, with a certain history and motivation—who commit the decisive acts or throw off the reins.

In the comparison with an army in action there is one important difference: a military unit does not consist of a fortuitous collection of individuals milling around, or a mass without responsible and action-orientating leadership. It consists of an organization and it is in the structure of that organization that we can find the differentiation and dynamics of violence.

Police violence. If technical violence is directed against objects (buildings, concentrations) and infantry violence against physically present armed opponents, what then should we imagine police violence to be?

Taken in a strict sense the police in a modern society do not recognize "enemies" and even less so are they intent on destroying enemies, as is the regular order of military men in battle situations. The police think far more in terms of public order, defined in a formal way, and its protection by the preparation of the legal prosecution and arrest of those intent on violating this public order. Hence police action is, by definition, discriminative in a positive sense; not "against" but "for" the people and, in the protection of that people, anti those who "break the law". This selectivity is found not only in the choice of those who are prosecuted (criminals, suspects, etc.) but also in the choice of the means, through which the attempt is made, to obtain a minimal exertion of violence and by which the desirable reaction to resistance is, as far as possible, "gentle persuasion."

The police deal primarily with suspects and people arrested. Such persons engage police attention because of a suspected or actually observed violation of norms. One of the main tasks of the police is to acquire as much information as possible about this violation of norms; criminality is systematically catalogued (on cards). Further steps against suspects and others are possible on the basis of this information.

> We see here a difference between those arrested by the police and prisoners of war. The military prisoner is an enemy rendered harmless, the person arrested by the police is a violator of norms, a suspect.

However, this picture is still rather incomplete and, moreover, of a recent date. Police repression was for a long time a weapon in the hands of social elites. The police did not only act selectively against criminal elements but also against social classes which endangered the desired balance of power.

If such groups and currents develop in contemporary society, the police react by the creation of a "special branch" which is empowered, because of special circumstances to undertake special measures. A "static" maintenance of order is no longer enough. One has to try to stop—in a dynamic way—a process. Police-organization then takes a special form.

> One form of this, and not even the most important, is the formation of riot police, ambulance brigades, police troups or whatever name is chosen for an organization which brings the police into the streets with helmets, eye-protectors, shields and with horses, motorbikes, black marias and water-cannon. The military model of violence is now closely approached: massive violence increases, selective violence decreases.

Even more radical is action by abolishing the right to hold meetings and have voluntary associations, directed against certain groups, by screening applicants for government functions, by massive arrests of people on the basis of membership of certain groups or the suspected existence of certain political sympathies.

It is exactly this type of police repression which in Indonesia became the task of the army as well as the police. The distance between the police and certain groups of the population now becomes a distance from the population in general. As long as the alarm system works, anybody who does not fulfill his duty of informing on guerillas or who offers help to the enemy or is politically suspect, is an object of police interference. When the alarm system is undermined by successful infiltration then police action is insufficient and becomes naked military violence. Houses of suspects are burned down, citizens are killed, third degree interrogations used on citizens even when it is in no way clear that they belong to the enemy camp—they could be enemies since there is no method left for distinguishing between guerillas and citizens.

Two developments are always seen going together: the increasing lack of control over an area and the increasing autonomy of specialized police violence. But this violence is in the final analysis also the expression of the power struggle and the ideology of the colonial elite. It is a desperate effort by the military authority to keep the situation under control, the communications intact and the plantations and other economic objects accessible. It is also justified by a traditional colonial-political ideology, according to which the population is "goodwilling", so that one only has to get bad elements under control.

According to this formula, on which all police action of the Dutch troops was based, guerillas who were incendiaries could be executed on the spot. The same line of behavior was followed as regards attacks on village heads cooperating with the Dutch administration, and the requisitions of rice and money by a local guerilla who functioned as a link in the military infiltration efforts of the enemy. This action which was called police action could only grow into repression of a military and political kind. The main role in this game was allotted to the military intelligence services. For us it is of primary importance how these services digested and treated the large members of arrested people, concretely: to what extent this sort of police activity degenerated into police violence and excessive violence.

With this we have also answered the question initially posed about the character of police violence in the strict sense: it is that violence directed against prisoners and arrestees who fell into the hands of the military intelligence service.

This intelligence service was an integral part of the army, necessary for obtaining information by techniques which varied from aerial reconnaissance and the decodification of enemy messages to the interrogation of prisoners.

This last source of information is still the most important as far as the movements of the enemy are concerned. It certainly became a cornerstone of the contra-guerilla. It offered, however, because of the reasons mentioned, a very great chance for the abuse of violence, now directed not only against the prisoners of war but also against citizens.

> A Dutch officer wrote us: "My experiences in interrogations by the German SD, later in those of the American intelligence service (1st Div. Aachen), in 1944, and the English Field Security in 1944/45 are identical. It is ironical that the Geneva Convention emphatically protects prisoners of war as far as interrogations are concerned whereas no single information service 'sticks' to it. It is also ironical that those who, like myself, had had personal experience of German interrogation methods and were determined that such a thing should never occur again saw more examples during our liberation and were later, in Indonesia, to apply the same methods" (personal communication).

We can mention in addition that part of the Dutch intelligence service personnel received its training in England and was there taught the techniques of interrogation which were later to be applied. According to at least one source third degree methods were declared to be admissible there, provided that traces of maltreatment were no longer visible two days after.

The use of torture did not occur to the same extent with all the ID, IVG—and NEFIS groups (various branches of Dutch intelligence services). Much depended on factors like the degree of autonomy and self-imposition of task, on training and selection.

In the early divisions overseas the ID was weakly developed at the lower levels; here the combat platoon operated without any specialized intelligence section. There was, however, an approach towards this in the institution of so-called "interpreters" in the first detachments of the Dutch East Indian Army. In the beginning the main task of these employees, who were always Indonesian, was indeed translation for intelligence tasks, especially for troops with no knowledge of the local languages; but they were soon involved in the exertion of police powers. Yet their tasks were very different. Some had only administrative functions in the improvisatorial ID-groups, others could be used for all kinds of things.

We said earlier that not only selection and professional tough-ening-up played a role, but also the forces of circumstances and opportunity. A "tough" group could, for instance, under quiet condi-tions behave in a very controlled manner whereas a "soft" group could act very harshly under difficult circumstances.

The modulations implicit in the system were conducive to a moving border.

This holds to a certain extent for all third degree interrogations because they function within the same changing complex of factors: the term "third" is relative. We find here undressing, beatings, string-ing up in awkward positions, electric torture, water torture, cigarette burns, shooting beside the head and—often because of lack of accommodation—agonizing isolation. These methods are so often mentioned in detail in the standard stories of the troops in Indo-nesia that one, in spite of the exaggeration and stereotyping, does not have to doubt the extent of these abuses. On the troop-transport ships going home these things were the subject of conversation and argument often ending in the unanimous comment that there was no need to reproach the Jerries.

One of the authors (H) who, as an outsider (signal man) got to know some local ID (intelligence) groups and was a few times present at interrogations, describes his experiences as follows:

> The interrogations took place with a certain formalism. The commander was often seated behind a little table, whereas it was usually Indonesian henchmen who had to do the dirty work. The scene made one think of old pictures of torture: the torturers rough and proletarian, the inquisitor observer having a certain gentility.

> The interrogations often started with friendliness. Only after the prisoner had "closed-up" would the Indonesian henchman start beating him with a stick and utter threats. Then the electrical current inductor was used first connected to fingers and toes; the real third-degree interrogation started when the prisoner was exhausted; the electrical wires were then transferred to the genitals. Some of the interrogated then lost consciousness.

> This kind of torture is for the ID-people a less physical affair than the real beatings. Continuous face-to-face contact is not necessary with this. One is only really angry when one is beating up the person under interrogation because the very action of doing this induces feelings of anger.

During electric torture the interrogated person often secretes urine or faeces, a thing which leads to suppressed laughter behind his back. The interrogations were intended to lead to the exhaustion of the tortured man, in the hope that this would make him betray his fellows. Often, however, he closed-up. An Indonesian experiences being manhandled as an insult the sense of being insulted makes him keep quiet out of pride.

The ID often tried to keep up a certain appearance of heroism, also out of pride. There is, for example, the well known "gun on the table" story: the commander puts a loaded gun on the table and tells the prisoner to shoot him down if he thinks he is a criminal.

One also heard stories everywhere about very clever interrogation methods which did not imply violence—a thing which was impossible in many ID-departments, was it only because of their very inadequate command of the language? There is a general tendency to pose as a "special department" which, of course, disposes of certain "special skills".

In fact, outsiders were kept at a distance. Their presence during interrogations made those being interrogated nervous: the system was interrupted. Sometimes one tried to put them out, sometimes to involve them in the self-justification which had been built up in the course of time. It was rather uncommon for an ordinary soldier to enter the room during an interrogation. Most soldiers tended to avoid the interrogation room.

Since the Dutch broadcasts and the Governmental Nota of 1969 —drawing on military archives—it has become unnecessary to add new, separate facts to the existing material. It would be far more important to know accurately how frequently such excesses occurred. This however, is a fact which could only be established with great difficulty as the ID liked to isolate itself from the ordinary troops and preferred to be kept in that isolation.

It is, however, certain that the Governmental Nota of 1969 gives a totally inaccurate picture of the situation. It is conspicuous that most complaints concern (except for the Special Forces) the alleged or established excesses committed by the intelligence services.[22] Furthermore, it is conspicuous in the Nota that many excesses never reached the military courts. This can be shown by an analysis of the facts.[23]

In the Nota, 110 cases are mentioned which concern physical assault, murder, manslaughter and serious or light maltreatment. If we isolate from these 19 sexual crimes, 11 cases of robbery and five cases in which the motives are not clear, then there remain 75 cases which have an obvious relation to the military function. Among these are 54 cases of murder or manslaughter. If we separate from these 9 cases in which it is clear that we are dealing with personal or mixed motives, then there remains 45 cases (60%) of murder or manslaughter, in which it is clear that we are dealing with police actions.

There are 6 cases in which prisoners died as the consequence of an interrogation. There are 12 cases in which prisoners were killed and 3 (not included in the 45) in which people were induced to do so, in all these cases by those who exercised direct authority over their prisoners. There are 9 cases in which this authority is not clear, but in which the killing took place under the motivation that one was dealing here with very suspicious persons; soldiers had been out looking for these people. Finally there are 10 cases of citizens dying as a consequence of "trigger-happiness."

If we limit ourselves to maltreatment, then we find 11 cases in which this took place during interrogations, whereas in 7 cases a reference is made to "suspicious behavior." In 1 of these 7 cases one can speak of an abuse of authority. If we now try to find out which of these cases were regarded by the military courts as being related to the exercise of police functions, we are in for a surprise. In *one* of these cases a NEFIS-officer (political intelligence branch) is mentioned (1-13: death of prisoner) and in one case an IVG-group (field intelligence) (1-28: death of seven prisoners). In one case a prisoner dies because of action by a soldier who offered help to a CP-group (general police-reserve) In the three cases of inducement to the killing of prisoners no link was laid with an ID-group. The military courts appear to have been chronically blind to actions by the ID and IVG.

If we now pay attention to the destruction of property, then it appears that in the 110 cases there was one case of this kind and here it was a matter of personal revenge. If we place this against the background of the habit of putting houses on fire by way of police action the strong impression arises that the military could commit no sin on this point as far as the military courts were concerned. The destruction of houses is not mentioned at all. Also, the technical cases of excess of violence, in cases of "trigger-happiness" in ordinary infantry action as well as in the use of heavy arms led in no single case to court action.

Police-military violence. We have seen thus far how the means for police action became a specialism built into the military apparatus. Now we will direct our attention to the fusion of political and military elements, which we shall describe under the name of the INCO-group (INtelligence-COmmand).

In this construction the intelligence-group does not function separately. Via the military commander a link is laid with the formal organization, via this cooperation police activities are legitimated: both parties constitute each other's cover-up. Because parts of the ordinary troops become involved in this transgression of norms, they are compromised and a "clique" originates. Reports then start to show a considerable discrepancy with the real events.

When this structure grows, the demolition of the system of norms also gains significance in the barracks. There it was still unclear who was actually the enemy in this unseen guerilla. In the original picture he was a military opponent conceived of as being more or less akin to the Japanese. Now there is also the citizen. At first one could take a purely military attitude; now one has to undertake police action as well. The INCO-group does the work, it is tolerated by the others and once these are compromised they contribute to keeping the improvised solutions secret.

This explains the mechanism around the task of area-control. Against the Indonesian citizen now stands military and police prestige and the escape provided by the formula of special circumstances. When the circumstances are repeated the INCO-group gains local recognition.

The INCO-group then functions in the region as a junta, which in spite of minimal professional skills and responsibility yet offers a solution, a local solution. It is then no longer surprising that very personal opinions are developed regarding affairs of area control which are normally in the hands of professional institutions such as the civil service, the courts and the police. These opinions show a mixture of military toughness—especially when the situation gets out of hand—and police intentions, especially in attempts to separate the enemy from the ordinary citizen.

We cite here one case from the governmental Nota of 1969: [24] An army sergeant shot and killed on the 29 March 1939 seven Indonesian prisoners and left them lying in the market place. In the place where this happened

(Djombang, East Java) there were many resistance fighters who set houses afire, and who plundered and abducted citizens; the sergeant thought that he, in his function as commander of a local intelligence group, should do something against these methods by setting an example.

A case from our own materials. On the 20 January 1949 a police inspector, together with an army sergeant and three sharp-shooters, went in a jeep to a sugar factory situated in a region in Middle Java, where a meeting was to take place with members of the "stormpolice" concerning actions there.

On the road they met five Indonesians, the inspector stopped and asked for their identification cards. These turned out to be in order. At that moment a man came along on a push bike. He was fairly well dressed and had no valid identification card with him. He claimed to come from a village nearby but did not know the name of the village-head there.

The inspector ordered the man to walk in front of him, drew his pistol and shot him in the neck. He ordered the five Indonesians to bring the corpse to the *assistent-wedana* (district chief).

Later in the day the inspector discussed the case with this *assistent-wedana* and subsequently made inquiries in the village which his victim had mentioned. When he came back he told that the man had been seen there the night before but was not a regular inhabitant. He gave the village-head five guilders to bury the man.

However, according to further information obtained from the sharp-shooters present the gist of the event as related here is true, but the details were different. A, one of the three sharp-shooters, claims that he also looked at the identification card the man showed; this document he says, was very obviously self-produced and very clumsily so. According to him it is not true either that the inspector shot the man without any further ado. He had originally wanted to make the man walk to the village to confirm his story there. When the man started walking, says A, we started to regret that we had let him go. The inspector then shot but did not kill him. A then gave him the final coup de grace, though sharp-shooter B at first tried to prevent him from doing this. C, who gave the story in the version we related above, could, according to A, not have seen this because he had remained behind at the decisive moment and stood with his back to the scene.

We give so much attention to one isolated incident because it reveals, within a small scope, the operation of an INCO-group in detail. The inspector was a popular figure with the soldiers. He always knew what to do in difficult situations and had at various times acted very decisively in dangerous situations.

He therefore had the edge on the sergeant from whom such action could not be expected as a self-evident matter. Sharp-shooter A identified with the Inspector.

> He says: I saw myself that the man's papers were no good. And: "we" regretted that we let the man go. He prides himself on the toughness shown by him. When he is confronted by our source (informant) with Sniper (sharpshooter) C, who was of the opinion that the inspector shot the man, he is indignant: "But I have done that." And to our source (informant): "you probably don't approve of that, but I fired that shot. B said to me: don't do it." Later, during guard duty, he remarked: "there are those boys who can't gun down people. To me it's all the same."

A's behavior is not exceptional. At another occasion he asked for permission to kill a wounded man, who was found after a gun-battle at a village edge. This permission was not granted; the wounded man was carried off and died on the way. B was of another calibre: he tried to stop A. Finally, C did not belong to the small group around the inspector. He did not quickly take the initiative and in this case too he was hardly interested.

He was present but hardly noticed what happened. His comment on the incident was: "It's not any of my business."

The picture is clear. The inspector, who had the reputation of reacting swiftly and adequately under all circumstances, made use of a broad mandate. The sergeant approved of this, and one of the sharp-shooters actually helped the inspector. The others were observers, with different feelings on the matter. Even in such a small group there is, together with a formal distribution of competence, also a personal accent. But the personal emphasis is set within the frame-work of the INCO-group, in which this drama took place.

In the above, we paid attention to the function of a specialization in violence and the excess of violence in newly-won regions, where control over the population has been lost. The data which are available concerning the infantry company studied in detail permit a certain quantitative test of both ways of explanation. See for this Table 1.

In the study of the figures presented these two warnings are in order. In the first place it is not a foregone conclusion that control of an area via an ID intelligence network involves more excesses of violence than alternative systems. Troops with no substantial intelligence service will no doubt also have indulged in tough, wrathful

Table 1

Survey of house-burnings by a Dutch infantry company, during the period
January 1948 to August 1949

Additional clarification
Only those cases have been mentioned which were compiled by the authors.
In all cases houses were set afire in the presence of the combat unit. Sometimes this was done by order from the commander, sometimes on the initiative
of the intelligence unit allocated to the company. In no case was the motive for
setting houses afire the clearing of a free field of fire.

Key:
A = situated within the alarm region (less than 5 kms. from the detachment).
B = on the border of the alarm region.
C = in newly taken-over regions, often when the local population was fleeing.
If other companies participated in the action, in addition to the company
concerned, the number of totally burned-down houses is divided according to
company.

Time	Number of Houses			Clarification
	A	B	C	

Period before the Second Action (1948)

Time	A	B	C	Clarification
June	1			House of an arrested person
July			30	Some houses set afire, after which others caught fire
Sept.	2			Houses of arrested persons

Period following the Second Action (1949)

Time	A	B	C	Clarification
Jan.			3 (a)	Fire contact during patrol. Effort of intelligence unit to set several dozens of houses afire foiled by rain
			60	In a troublesome region. Three days before one Dutch soldier killed, three wounded
			8	Same day
			2	With the help of petrol
			20	Incidental cases in same combat region
Feb.			2	Same village as under (a)
			100	400 houses set afire by 4 companies during mopping up actions in reconquered territory
April	4			1 house set afire; other houses also caught fire. People had the idea that they had spotted guerilla fighters; no fire contact; population fled at approach of patrol
May			2	Same village as under (a)
June			10	Action outside company territory

Table 1 (*continued*)

July	200	800 houses by 4 companies, during action outside company territory. Three villages burned down in total

Data concerning enemy reprisals

Within the company's territory a school, on the border of the alarm system, was burned down at the end of 1948, and in August 1949 another school outside this system. In December 1948 ten houses were burned down during an infiltration of the TNI. After the Dutch retreat from an outpost the houses there and in the environment were burned down by Indonesian guerilla-fighters. During that period a lurah and an assistant village head were assassinated by guerilla fighters.

In the total area of the batallion 400 houses were burned down within the alarm systems and about ten persons assassinated, all of whom had cooperated with the Dutch intelligence service with the exception of a village head— appointed by the ID but passive—and the wife of a village head who was missing.

Survey of excesses in use of arms and during interrogations by a Dutch infantry company in the period January 1948 to August 1949

Categories:

A = killing of prisoners by ID-groups. (Note that only in the December-case is there no connection with the ID.)

B = killing of civilians.

C = shooting civilians.

D = third degree interrogations by the ID in separate rooms within the barracks.

E = third degree interrogations by the ID during patrol-action.

The company concerned is described in greater depth in Chapter V. Cases of civilian casualties during first contact with a recognizable military opponent are not included.

Time	*Number of Victims*					*Elucidation*
	A	B	C	D	E	
whole period				X		Number of arrests at least 400 to 500 with mainly third degree interrogations
April/ Aug. '49	Z					According to various and divergent statements between "several dozens" and "several hundreds." After infiltration and during mopping up operations in the company's territory of 300km^2 of mountainous terrain, a concentration of villages of more than 100,000 people. Strength of local Dutch forces: two platoons

Table 1 (*continued*)

Time	A	B	C	D	E	Elucidation
1948						
Aug.		1				Shooting on command, obeyed by four soldiers
	1					Unnecessary shooting on command of an escaped prisoner
					6	During patrol
Sept.		1				Prisoner found dead in his cell; cause obscure
Oct.		1				Prisoner taken from cell and killed during patrol; an attempt to escape merely being the alleged motive, according to many witnesses
Dec.		1				Prisoner killed under obscure circumstances by an accident with a weapon
					4	During patrol
1949						
Jan.		1				Civilian wounded during attempt to flee, killed by commanding officer
				2		
Feb.		1				After interrogation
	1					Former ID-agent who tried to flee arrested and executed
March			1			Shot woman left behind severely wounded
				2		
					2	
Aug.		1				Prisoner killed in presence of patrol

or panicky reactions. The ID constituted at least an attempt to provide an adequate response to the guerilla. Where this was lacking pointless violence could easily take its place.

In the second instance it is not possible to generalize. It is far from improbable that the infantry company concerned—at any case as regards the character of the incidents—had an above average score in these matters. This can not be proved as the data are insufficient: it is, however, a fact that this company constituted an exception within the batallion in which it operated alongside other companies. On the other hand, this company had to maintain itself in circumstances which were not dissimilar to those prevailing for a great number of other Dutch detachments. One can only fear that these matters also got "out of hand."

POINT OF NO RETURN

It could happen that prisoners were so badly maltreated during their first interrogation that they could not be transferred to a higher echelon, which was often the order. People feared difficulties, "troublesome" questions, perhaps criticism or even a report and a court case. In those cases prisoners were liquidated.

This solution had symbolic significance for the entire situation of the troops in Indonesia after World War II. It was at the basis of the organization, in the smallest units of intelligence groups, in remote detachments, on inland-patrols, in isolated combat units acting as the brigades of Special Forces that violence was committed. In the final analysis it was always an act committed by certain persons, by certain small groups, operating in a sphere of secrecy and isolation even when there was nothing to hide, in unclear situations, off the main road, outside the camp, in a confused clash, on their own initiative.

Often after what had happened, it could not be established with certainty whether events had been unavoidable or whether their course could and should have been different. The intelligence services consciously retreated into isolation and rationalized the hard line or tried to over-awe people in their environment with a show of factual knowledge and control of the situation. But even what happened on ordinary infantry patrols remained obscure to those who stayed behind, and sometimes even to some participants.

Reconstructions of events after they have occurred are always difficult; people put out various versions, often in good faith. There are lacunae in the story, often maintained on purpose.

The reports on the events in Indonesia were often written by those commanding posts and patrols. They give a reading of what happened which can not arouse criticism. One of the authors (J.v.D.) who, because of his function, had to read hundreds of patrol reports, never found a trace of excessive violence in these.

There are plenty of formulae available for clouding such behavior. These formulae—used in every war—were: shot while attempting to flee, or prisoner made a threatening gesture, grabbed his weapon, resisted arrest or even—said in all innocence: was impertinent. . . .

He who was not on the spot, cannot prove anything. It may have been true, was it only in the perception of the man firing the fatal shot? The others will not betray him; it might have happened to them as well.

A sergeant with five men is patrolling along a city edge, somewhere in Java. After returning to the camp he writes his report which is typed and signed by the commanding officer:

> At m.r. 711609 there was such an amount of light that it drew my attention and I decided to check up on it. When we forced our way into the house we found a man in the lighted room who sat down on the floor after he had initially refused to open the door.
> Subsequently he made an attacking movement with a bamboo spear lying beside him—this forced me to fire. The man was hit in the head and died instantly. From subsequent information we learned that the dead man was a well-known guerilla leader.

Under this report the sergeant wrote the place and date, and his signature. Behind the heading "ammunition used" he wrote: "One cartridge (pistol calibre 7.65)."

This patrol now has "a history;" the participants are known to have been involved in this event and they will keep quiet. Was the threatening gesture really made? Was the shooting necessary? Did it have to result in a killing? Was the man the leader of a guerilla group? Why then is his name not mentioned?

It may all have been true; who can tell? Perhaps the sergeant had an excellent record, perhaps he was dog-tired, or maybe he was a notorious figure in this detachment who had written more reports like these, but could not be missed; he may have been replacing an officer on sick-leave to Holland, he could have been one of the few still available for patrols. Who will judge? Not his commanding officer who has signed the report. He needs this sergeant and has promised him, after an exchange of words, to "shield" him once again.

In Indonesia every detachment had "a history." There were "platoon secrets," not open to outsiders, not even to personnel within the detachment such as people belonging to the signal service. In the last instance everyone had to shield himself.

Violence defends itself. A deed, once perpetrated, becomes a datum. People do not want to discuss it, they certainly do not want criticism.

Hofwijk, the newspaper reporter, popular with the men and fully sympathizing with them, one day finds members of the marines detachment with which he is staying, engaged in burning down houses around the detachment's position: free field of fire.

He wants to bring himself to understand this but yet finds that "people have been a bit too generous with matches."

Then he writes:

> I stood there listening for a few minutes to the bamboo which exploded with enormous bangs and, damnit, after some ten minutes I became so angry that I went right to the commanding officer and asked him whether this was all really necessary; when they made their positions in the middle of a village, too much was always destroyed, whereas perhaps they could have made their positions somewhat more to the outside. Certainly, some fifteen houses had been burned down.
>
> I knew in advance that he would not "take" it and when I asked him whether this was not all getting a bit out of hand, he gave me a real dressing-down. "You are a civilian, you think 'ethically'; I am a soldier, I think as a military man and I take all the measures which are required for the safety of my own people."
>
> We got into a fairly violent argument and after a few minutes he said: "I don't want to hear any more about it; I know your sort of people. Go and raise the hue and cry about it in Holland; that doesn't interest me a jot." At that moment I lost many friends . . . it was the first time that I saw hostile faces around me.[25]

The soldier resists his task and he resists it doubly when it is difficult to perform or when the people who initially give him his orders later thwart him in his attempt to carry these out.

That task is the control of territory with military means. Sometimes the soldier is successful; he gets hold of guerilla-leaders and sends these "higher-up" only to discover that there is a political agreement which leads to their extradition to the Republic.

A captain speaking:

> And then it doesn't take long before you see the same face in your area again. Liquidating them . . . certainly, that is the most efficacious way of going about it, but I feel little inclination to spend some years in prison here. . . . No, then we prefer to let these fellows go and wait until our time is up. A bad show, of course, but one is forced to do this.[26]

Not only the detachments, the whole army has a history. This holds most clearly for the volunteers, who signed up for the war against Japan and then were obliged to go to Indonesia. They came from liberated Holland and fondly believed that they could go and play the same role of liberation in the tropics. Immediately after arrival it turned out that things were not quite what they had expected.

A volunteer speaking: [27]

The soldiers (coming from Malaya, March 1946) spent an afternoon and a night in the transit camp near the harbor. This camp was controlled by a detachment of the British-Indian army, and there was a handful of Japanese prisoners of war who had to perform cleaning services.

When the soldiers arrived at the camp, they greeted the Indians in a comradely fashion, because in Malaya the relation with them had been very good. But things here were not what they were in Malaya. The Indians were full of cool reserve and one of them kept repeating "Dutchman no good," while a begloved Japanese sat smiling beside him on the balustrade.

The Dutch hadn't expected this at all and didn't quite know how to react.

The following day they went in a convoy, protected by tanks and airplanes, right through Batavia to Rawah-Bangka, on the South-Eastern edge of Meester Cornelis. The Dutch believed that they would be welcomed as liberators. When they drove into the city they cheered, they waved to the people and some of them scattered cigarettes as they had seen the allied troops do when they arrived in Holland as liberators. But the city looked empty, neglected and run-down and the few Indoesians who were in the streets did not react to the cheering. Some of them, who were standing in front of their huts ostentatiously turned their backs on us when the trucks approached, and some women kept their hand in front of the eyes of the baby in their arms.

That first day the trap of violence for the Dutch army was already there—wide open but still invisible. The stream of rationalizations would start to flow later in a desperate search for justification of the violence which was going to be used. Often people thought they were on firm ground, when they had restored order in a region and saw economic life beginning to flourish again, when they saw comrades helping the sick, when they discovered ordinary humanity in themselves and others. Sometimes too they thought they could see through to the end, to military successes: to Jogja and then home.

But the trap of violence turned out to be deeper than anyone could have guessed. Events progressed from the defence of positions to the First Action, from that Action via continuous mopping up operations to a fight against infiltrations and then to a new, a Second Action, and that was not the end either. Soldiers kept asking themselves what use was this adventure, which started in the offices and camps of the war volunteers, many inspired with the desire to oust the Japanese, and came to a dead end in remote detachments situated in guerilla territory.

NOTES

[1] For a striking example of this kind of interpretation, see: E. F. M. Durbin and John Bowlby, *Personal Aggressiveness and War* (London: Routledge & Kegan Paul, 1939, repr. 1950).

[2] J. W. Hofwijk, *Blubber* (Heemstede: De Toorts, 1948), 131.

[3] Jan Varenne, *Eer de haan kraait: Een serdadoe soesoe tussen de peloppers op. Java* (Amsterdam: Paris, 1969), 9.

[4] *Nota betreffende het archievenonderzoek naar gegevens omtrent excessen in Indonesië begaan door Nederlandse militairen in de periode 1945-1950* (The Hague: Staatsuitgeverij, 1969, Dutch government publication), appendix 5, 15-17.

[5] Hofwijk, *op. cit.*, 131.

[6] *Nederlands Indie 1945—Indonesië 1949—Achter het Nieuws 1969* (Publication Broadcast Association VARA, 1969), 11, 13, 17.

[7] H. J. van Mook, *Indonesië, Nederland en de wereld* (Amsterdam: Arbeiderspers, 1949), 134 f.

[8] *Nota betreffende het archievenonderzoek . . . , op. cit.*

[9] *Ibid.*, 7; appendix 12.

[10] Ernie Pyle, *Here is Your War* (Cleveland and New York: World Publ. Cy., 1945), 196.

[11] It is easy to see this from their way of reporting. See *Pioniers Overzee*: De geschiedenis van het bataljon Genietroepen van de Eerste Divisie '7 December' ('C' Divisie) 1945-1950 (n.d.).

[12] From: *Oefening op de Kaart 'B' Divisie* (Document from Territorial/Troop-Command Semarang, 28 October 1948, mimeograph).

[13] W. A. Schouten and H. B. Evers, 'Het gebruik van artillerie, ingedeeld bij de V-Brigade gedurende en na de politionele actie', *Militaire Spectator,* Vol. CXVIII (1949), 226.

[14] C. A. Heshusius, 'Het gebruik van tanks in Nederlands Indië', *Militaire Spectator,* Vol. CXVI (1947), 563, 717.

[15] *Artillerievuur in de Tropen*. Herinneringen aan het 8e Regiment Veldartillerie, 3e Inf. Brigade, C Divisie '7 December' (n.d., n.p.l.).

[16] Official reports Dutch East Indian Army.

[17] Schouten and Evers, *op. cit.*, 232.

[18] *Nota betreffende het archievenonderzoek . . . , op. cit.*

[19] A detailed analysis gives: F. Doeleman, *De medische geschiedenis van een infanterie-bataljon der Koninklijke Landmacht gedurende drie jaar actieve dienst op Java 1946-1950* (Assen: Van Gorcum—Hak & Prake, 1955), 165 ff.

[20] Hofwijk, *op. cit.*, 92.

[21] G. van Heek, *Front op Java: Mijn diensttijd in Indonesië 1947-1950* (Hengelo, 1952).

[22] Source: *Nota betreffende het archievenonderzoek . . . , op. cit.*, supplements 5, 20, 23, 26, 27, 31, 32, 39, 47.

[23] *Ibid.*, supplement 7.

[24] *Ibid.*, supplement 7, 7.

[25] Hofwlik, *op. cit.*, 178-80.

[26] A. van Sprang, *Laatste acte: Een cocktail van soldatenleven en politiek in Indonesië* (The Hague: Van Hoeve, 1949), 11 f.

[27] Diary, F. Grünfeld, Amsterdam.

177

Acknowledgements

ACKNOWLEDGEMENTS

I am grateful to the editors and publishers of the following publications in permitting me the use of articles and chapters that originally appeared in their pages.

The Genesis of Military and Industrial Organization is reprinted in part from: J. van Doorn, Organisatie en Maatschappij, pp. 207-26, copyright 1966 by H. E. Stenfert Kroese N.V., Leyden.

The Officer Corps: A Fusion of Profession and Organization, from Archives Européennes de Sociologie, Vol. VI (1965), pp. 262-82; abridged.

Political Change and the Control of the Military is an adapted reprint from Military Profession and Military Regimes, edited by Jacques van Doorn, pp. 11-31, copyright 1969 by Mouton & Co. N.V., The Hague.

Justifying Military Action: The Dutch Return to Indonesia 1945-1949, reprinted from On Military Ideology, edited by Morris Janowitz and Jacques van Doorn, pp. 77-95, copyright 1971 by Universitaire Pers Rotterdam.

Use of Violence in Counter Insurgency: The Indonesian Scene 1945-1949, is an adapted and abridged reprint of chapter IV from J. A. A. van Doorn and W. J. Hendrix, Ontsporing van geweld: Over het Nederlands/Indisch/Indonesisch conflict, pp. 171-220, copyright 1970 by Universitaire Pers Rotterdam.

The Decline of the Mass Army was presented as a contribution to the Amsterdam Conference of the Research Committee on Armed Forces and Society, International Sociological Association, in March 1973.

The Military and the Crisis of Legitimacy was presented to the Research Committee on Armed Forces and Society at the VIIth World Congress of Sociology, at Toronto, in August 1974.

In the course of my work in the fascinating field of the sociology of the military, I have become indebted to many people who have helped me in a variety of ways. I would like to thank especially Morris Janowitz, whose encouragement and guidance have been invaluable during the decade we have been acquainted.

Rotterdam

August 1974

J.v.D.

Index

INDEX

Academies, military   13 18 19 35 40
   75f
Africanization of the armed forces
   69f
Airforce   149ff
Aitken, H. G. J.   27
Alboldt, E.   27
Algeria   102 126
Alienation of the military   98f
Ambler, John Steward   106 132
American armed forces   13 19 51
American Revolution   95
Apter, David E.   86 94 106
Argentina   80
Artillery   9 17 18 145f 149ff
Atrocities   122f 133-176
   explanations   134ff
   parliamentary intervention   142f
   quantification   164f 169ff
   secrecy   172ff
Austria   15
Authority pattern   21f

Bahrdt, Hans-Paul   28
Ball-Rokeach, Sandra J.   89 105 107
Barry, Brian M.   106
Baynes, J. C. M.   106
Bédarida, François   46
Beishline, John R.   25
Belgium   52
Bell, Daniel   63
Bell, M. J. V.   85
Benda, Harry J.   132

Bendix, Reinhard   25 26 27
Biderman, Albert D.   63 107
Blau, Peter M.   45
Boulding, Kenneth E.   63 105
Bowlby, John   177
Brest van Kempen, C. P.   27
Britain, Great   7 8 19 52 104
British colonies   128
British intervention in Indonesia   11f
Bureaucratization   14
Business elite   13

Cabernard, P.   25
Capitalism and the military   10f 34
Cavalry   9 14 19
China, People's   51 55 67 68 73 76 77
Civilianization of the military   99
Colijn, H.   114 131
Company, early development   9 10
Comparative studies of the military
   25 (note 3)
Congo-Kinshasa   79
Conscription   54 56ff 96
Counter-insurgency   103, 117 133-176
Cressey, Donald R.   46
Cromwell   8
Cuba   55
Cvrcek, Jaromir   85 86
Czechoslovakia   69 70 71 75 76 77 81
   96

Decolonization   111-130
Demeter, Karl   26 27 46

185

Denmark   52
Deutsch, Karl W.   95 105
Dobratz, Betty A.   60 64
Doeleman, F.   177
Dogan, Mattei   26
Drees, W.   131
Droysen, G.   25
Dudley, B. J.   73 79 86
Durbin, E. F. M.   177
Durkheim, Emile   46
Dutch East Indies
   see: Indonesia
Dutch forces in Indonesia   111-130
Dutch Republic   8 11f

Eastern European countries   65-83
Easton, David   89 92 105
Eckstein, Harry   99 106
Effectiveness, concept of   93f
Engineering corps   9 17 18 145f 148ff
Enrolment patterns   57f
Etzioni, Amitai   45 92 105
Evan, William M.   25
Evers, H. B.   177
Expenditures, military   51f

Feld, M. D.   46 55
Feuilletau de Bruyn, W. K. F.   131
Finer, S. E.   46 59 64 79 83 85 86 97
   106
Foot, M. R. D.   63
France   11 13 51 52 81 98 102
Frederick the Great   15
French Revolution   13 54 95

Gadourek, I.   86
Gamson, William A.   105
Garthoff, Raymond L.   85 86
Gehlen, Arnold   105
Gerbrandy, P. S.   131
German Democratic Republic   70 71
   75
Germany   11 13 17 19 34 35 51 97 98
   99
Germany, National-Socialist   73 74 81
Gerretson, C.   131
Ghana   70 80
Ginsburg, Robert N.   46
Girardet, Raoul   26 46 86 132

Goffman, Erving   40 46
Gouldner, Alvin W.   45
Graczyk, Jozef   75 76 85 86
Grünfeld, F.   177
Grusky, Oscar   25 26
Guerrilla warfare   136 137 141 155ff
Gurr, Ted Robert   105
Gustavus Adolphus   33

Häckel, Erwin   63
Hahlweg, Werner   26 45
Harries-Jenkins, Gwyn   63
Hartmann, Heinz   45
Hatta, Mohammad   116
Helle, H. J.   26
Hendrix, W. J.   131
Heshusius, C. A.   177
Hierarchy, military   12 30f 37 135ff
Hofwijk, J. W.   135 158 174 177
Höhn, Reinhard   27
Holland   13 14 18 52 99 102
Homans, George Caspar   92 105
Hueting, J. E.   138
Hungary   102
Hunt, Kenneth   63
Huntington, Samuel P.   31 45 46 59
   64 81 83 86 95 97 105 106 132

Ideology
   and military intervention   113ff
   in the armed forces   72f
   latent   129
India   51
Indianization of the military   69 70
Indoctrination of armed forces   72f
   113ff
Indonesia   51 68 111-176
Industrial Revolution   10 17
Infantry   9 14 54 146f 153ff
Intelligence, military   140 162ff 164ff
   172
Intervention, military   78 113ff
Ireland, Northern   104
Isolation of the armed forces   59f
Israel   68 72 73
Italy   51

Jähns, M.   26
Jahn, Georg   27

Janowitz, Morris   25 26 27 28 45 46
    60 63 64 85 106 107 132
Japan   102
Japanese occupation of Indonesia   112
    115 116 118 119 121 122 124 125
    129
Joffe, Ellis   85 86
Johnson, John J.   85
Jongeneel, D. J.   131

Kaempffert, Waldemar   25
Kahin, George McTurnan   131
Kelly, George Armstrong   132
Kiès, Ch.   131
Kirchheimer, Otto   55 63
Kolkowicz, Roman   86
Korea   68 73 80
Kornhauser, William   63
Kourvetaris, George A.   60 64
Kroes, Rob   106 124 128 132

Lammers, C. J.   46 132
Lang, Kurt   27 55 63 81 86 98 106
Lasswell, Harold D.   39
Latin America   102
Lazarsfeld, Paul F.   25
Legitimacy
    as potentiality   91ff
    classification   90f
    concept of   88ff
    definition   89f
    of colonial rule   116f
    of the military   87-104
Lewis, Michael   27 45 46
Lipset, Seymour Martin   89 94 105
Litwak, Eugene   99 106
Lijphardt, Arend   132
Loewe, Victor   46
Luhmann, Niklas   105

Malaya   175
Manpower, military   51f
Mans, Jan H.   106
Marx, Karl   26 60
Mass army   22 51-61
Maurice of Orange   11f 14f 26 33
Mazrui, Ali A.   67 80 85 86
Mercenary armies   9 15 33
Merton, Robert K.   25 45

Meyer, H. J.   106
Meyer-Welcker, Hans   86
Meynaud, Jean   26
Middle Ages   8
Military Revolution   17 32f 35
Militarization of politics   97f
Moskos Jr., Charles C.   63 99 106 132
Muso rebellion in Indonesia   121f

Nation in Arms   53 54
Navy   15 17 19 34
Netherlands, the
    see: Holland
Nettl, J. P.   91 105
Neundörfer, Ludwig   27 28
Nigeria   68 70
Nobility in the armed forces   9 12 13
    14 19 35f 38 70
Norway   52

Officer corps   29-43
Organization, formal
    comparative studies   7ff
    as a construction   5
    as a grouping   6
    as a social institution   6
    definition   5-7 32
    genesis   11ff 32ff
Organization, industrial   9-23
Organization, military   29-43 144ff
Otley, C. B.   85

Paret, Peter   107
Parsons, Talcott   29 90 105
Paternalism in the armed forces   15,
    19
Paterson, T. T.   25
Pauker, Guy J.   85
Phelps Brown, E. H.   25
Picard, H. W. J.   131
Poland   69 70 71 73 74
Police operations   159ff 166ff
Political commissars   74
Political control of the armed forces
    65-83
    erosion of control   75ff
    indoctrination   72f
    organization   73f

purges 69f
recruitment and selection 70f
Political culture, level of 79 82
Politicization of the armed forces 41 42 65-83 96
Popitz, Heinrich 27
Popular sovereignty 97
Portugal 102
Poten, B. 46
Price, James L. 105 106
Professionalism, military 12 14 29-43 59 75f 80ff
definition 34ff
Professionalization of the officer corps 34ff
Proletarization of the officer corps 70 76 77
Protestant Ethic 8
Prussia 8 15 19 35 96
Pyle, Ernie 147 177

Radway, Laurence I. 106
Rank structure 20
Rapoport, David C. 88 105
Rau, Günter 85 86
Recruitment and selection 70f
Redlich, Fr. 27 45 46
Roberts, Adam 107
Roberts, Michael 25 26 27 45 46
Roethlisberger, F. J. 27
Rose, Richard 105
Russia, 19th century 69f

Scandinavian countries 99
Schmückle, Gerd 45
Schouten, W. A. 177
Schulze, Karl-Heinz 85 86
Scientific management 11
Scott, W. Richard 45
Self-recruitment of officers 13
Shanas, E. 106
Short Jr., James F. 105
Sills, David L. 105
Size of armed forces 52 54
Sjahrir, Sutan 116
Slamet, Mas 131
Smelser, Neil J. 25
Social origin of the military 13f 38f 71 76f

Socialization, military 144ff
Sohn, Jae Souk 68 80 85 86
Solomon, D. N. 28
Somer, J. M. 132
Soviet Union 51 67 68 69 72 73 76 77 81 116
Spanish Civil War 102
Special Forces 141 154 164 172
Speier, Hans 8 25 101 106
Sternberger, Dolf 89 105
Stouffer, Samuel A. 27 28
Streib, F. G. 106
Stüber, Erwin 85 86
Sukarno 116
Sweden 8 33

Tanzania 67 68 70 79
Tax, Sol 63 105
Taylor, Frederick Winslow 11f 14f 27 33
Technical revolution in armed forces and industry 16ff
Teitler, Ger 53 63 106
Thompson, James D. 105
Torture 162ff 170f
Turkey 51

Uganda 70
United Nations 125
United States 52 54 58 102 122

Van den Heuvel, M. 131
Van Doorn, Jacques 25 26 45 64 85 86 106 107 131 132
Van Heek, G. 177
Van Mook, Hubertus J. 131 140 177
Van Poll, M. 131
Van Sprang, Alfred 177
Van Wulfften Palthe, P.M. 131
Varenne, Jan 135 177
Vietnam 80 102 126 153
Vietnam, North 73
Vinke, P. 26 27
Violence 133-176
infantry 153ff
police 159ff
police-military 166ff
technical 148ff
typology 100ff 144ff

Volunteer armed forces 56ff
Von Frauenholz, Eugen   25 26 27 45
    46

War criminality
    see: atrocities
Warfare, types of   101
Weber, Max   8 10 25 26 34 45 89 91
    105
Welch, C. J.   106

Westerling, Raymond   123
Wiatr, Jerzy J.   71 85
Wilensky, Harold L.   45, 46
Wijn, J. W.   25 26 27
Wolfgang, Martin E.   105
Wool, Harold   54 63
World War I, II   54 55 111f

Zhilin, P.   76 86
Zolberg, Aristide A.   68 73 79 85

Jacques van Doorn is Professor of Sociology in the Department of Social Science, Erasmus University, Rotterdam. Since 1974 he has been Chairman of the Research Committee on Armed Forces and Society of the International Sociological Association.

His primary interests are in the field of sociology of organizations, and in political and military sociology. He is the author of a number of sociological works in Dutch, and has contributed articles to international journals and readers. He is the editor of *Armed Forces and Society: Sociological Essays* (1968), *Military Profession and Military Regimes: Commitments and Conflicts* (1969), and in collaboration with Morris Janowitz, of *On Military Intervention* (1971), and *On Military Ideology* (1971).